MISSIONS IN CRISIS

Also by Eric S. Fife

A Highway for our God: The Christian's missionary responsibility in the light of God's purpose for the world.

MISSIONS IN CRISIS

Rethinking Missionary Strategy

by

ERIC S. FIFE

ARTHUR F. GLASSER

With a Foreword by

J. OSWALD SANDERS

LONDON

INTER-VARSITY FELLOWSHIP

39 BEDFORD SQUARE, W.C.1

First British Edition July 1962
Reprinted December 1963

*Printed in Great Britain by
Fletcher & Son Ltd, Norwich*

Contents

Part III.   The Church on the Offensive

Foreword

THE CRISIS facing the missionary enterprise today is so patent as to need no elaboration. In a contemporary missionary study it is affirmed that "we find ourselves in a dynamic society in which rapid change goes on at an unprecedented pace in almost all areas of life. Man finds himself in a situation in which he must make a fast-moving succession of decisions, momentous in their depth and dimension." It is the fierce blowing of these winds of change that makes imperative a radical reappraisal of the whole missionary situation. This the authors of this volume aim to do.

The book is admittedly controversial, but if it succeeds in stimulating serious thought on missionary themes of paramount importance, it will perform a much needed service. The approach is realistic, and pertinent to the world ferment of our times. Some prevailing missionary viewpoints and practices are sharply challenged.

5

A revision of priorities is suggested. Poignant lessons are adduced from China's travail, and while they may not meet with universal acceptance, the general deductions are too obvious to be ignored.

The penetrating analysis of Communism and its impact on missions by one who lived for some time under its yoke, will be of great value to those working in lands already threatened by this totalitarian tyranny. It is convincingly urged that disquieting trends in the ecumenical movement, the significant shift of population from country and provincial centres to swollen cities, the staggering challenge of vast student bodies in universities and colleges, alike demand a courageous revision of mission policy and strategy.

Few will wish to challenge the conclusion that there must be an earnest attempt to mobilise the resources of the whole Church in the spiritual warfare in which she is engaged, if her missionary responsibility is ever to be discharged.

It will readily be seen that the book is written with the American scene and the American public in view, hence the statistics and illustrations are drawn from that context. Much of the material presented arose out of student discussions and is slanted to that constituency. But while all that is written may not be relevant in detail to the British or the European scene, the underlying principles are of general application, and the discriminating reader will not miss the message of the book.

J. Oswald Sanders

Preface

I<small>N</small> 1954 DAVID ADENEY, then Missionary Director of the Inter-Varsity Christian Fellowship, directed the first Missionary Camp for students and graduates at Cedar Campus, an I.V.C.F. camp in northern Michigan. The program consisted of a balanced diet of practical evangelism in surrounding villages, lectures on missionary subjects, and devotional talks and studies.

In the years that this Missionary Camp has been operating, a stream of young people have passed through and have found their way into various types of Christian service in North America and many countries throughout the world. It has been our privilege to be associated with the Missionary Camp for a number of years. We have benefited beyond measure from our fellowship with the distinguished missionary leaders who have lectured at the camp and also by exposure to the splendid young people who have been so eager in their devotion to the Lord and penetrating in their questions concerning missionary work.

Much of the thinking expressed in this book has been stimulated by the questions asked by these young people, and we dedicate it to those graduates of Missionary Camp who are serving God in countries throughout the world.

ERIC S. FIFE
ARTHUR F. GLASSER

Introduction: Age of Crisis

W<small>HOEVER AMONG US</small> longs for a quiet life," Leon Trotsky once observed, "has certainly chosen the wrong epoch." To the present inhabitants of our planet, crises are like familiar possessions. World statesmen live with crises that mount in complexity. Newspapers blacken their pages with them, daily conveying their varying details in towering bold type. For ours is an age of crisis, of culminating upheavals, of constantly accelerating inner and outer revolutions in all phases of life.

Crises, however, are not necessarily bad, much less fatal. By definition a crisis is a crucial time and a turning point, the outcome of which determines the consequences that follow. Both Calvary and Pentecost may be defined as crises in the affairs of God and the world. The result of a crisis can be life or death, good or evil, freedom or slavery, victory or defeat, growth or sterility.

We are living in a time of unparalleled crisis in world

9

affairs; a period when crises have developed in every corner of the globe. The year 1945 signalled the end of one titanic power struggle and the arrival of another. Seemingly irrepressible and volatile forces have perpetuated a succession of unbroken crises which have undermined the complacency of almost every nation. Such phrases as cold war, hot war, nuclear deterrent, iron and bamboo curtain countries, containment, and peaceful co-existence on one hand, and nationalism, independence, revolution, subversion, reform, revolt, riot, racism, and persecution on the other have become commonplace in our vocabulary. In the wake of an outmoded colonialism, a host of newly independent nations, many of them premature, have reared their proud young heads—and not without travail. The partition of the sub-continent of India, the revolution and civil war in China—each were excruciatingly painful processes for any nation to go through. Sometimes the outcome of this struggle, this crisis, has been a happy one—sometimes tragically unhappy.

Communism has ridden this revolutionary upheaval to its own advantage. More particularly since the death of Stalin, communism has readopted Leninist principles in exploiting conditions, especially nationalism, in the underdeveloped countries. Today Marxism has enslaved one-third of the population of the world under a system which not only professes atheism, but is bent on the destruction of the Church as a spiritual force. Yet as Britain's Foreign Secretary, Lord Home, stated in

June, 1961, at Harvard's 310th commencement: "There is nothing inevitable in the progress of communism. It will advance or be defeated in proportion to the virility of the philosophy and the way of life which opposes it."

These and many other exterior tensions have affected in greater or lesser degree the missionary task of the Church—sometimes in a tragic manner as with the Church in China in the communist take over in 1949. By themselves, these factors would be enough to justify the title, "Missions in Crisis." But there have also been tensions within, as well as pressures without.

The Church today finds herself in the midst of a turbulent and protracted theological crisis. William Richey Hogg, in his definitive account of the development of the ecumenical movement, points out:

> . . . the early 1920's brought a particularly acute division among many Protestants. The basic conflict concerned the verbal inspiration and infallibility of the Bible. . . . The nature of the conflict was divisive, sectarian, and exclusive. It led some groups to withdraw from common ventures.[1]

The 1930's and 1940's saw a new development in the theological tension as the influence of Barth and Brunner made itself felt. Bultmann, although a contemporary of Barth and Brunner, has taken much longer to make his voice widely heard, but his more radical views, together with those of Tillich, are in the ascendancy in

1. *Ecumenical Foundations* (New York: Harper & Brothers, 1952), p. 216.

11

the theological crisis of our day. The wide divergence of theological views and their implications for foreign missions are evident in the recent publication, *The Theology of the Christian Mission*, edited by Gerald H. Anderson.[2]

The Church finds herself involved not only in fierce theological debate (some would say decline), but equally momentous, in a state of ecclesiastical flux. Since World War II, the birth and growth of the World Council of Churches has been most notable. Originally stemming, to a large extent, from the missionary activity of the Church both before and since the Edinburgh Congress of World Missions in 1910, this trend has now resulted in the assimilation of the International Missionary Council within the World Council of Churches. Missionaries in denominational, interdenominational, and nondenominational societies have found themselves with sharply divided views on the many issues involved in this merger.

A bishop of the postwar constituted Church of South India, Lesslie Newbigin, discussing the two main streams of Christianity, Catholicism and Orthodox Protestantism, has pointed out: "It is necessary, however, to recognize that there is a third stream of Christian tradition which, though of course mingling at many points with the other two, has yet a distinct character of its own. It is important to recognize this fact because *this stream at present runs more outside of than inside of the ecumenical movement* and has so far taken an in-

2. New York: McGraw-Hill Book Company, 1961.

adequate part in the theological encounter which that movement has made possible"[3] [italics ours]. Newbigin characterizes this stream by saying that "its central element is the conviction that the Christian life is a matter of the experienced power and presence of the Holy Spirit today; that neither orthodoxy of doctrine nor impeccability of succession can take the place of this."[4]

It is significant that while the World Council of Churches is often regarded as the voice of Protestant Christianity, over sixty per cent of all Protestant foreign missionaries in the world serve with missions that are unaffiliated, even indirectly, with the World Council of Churches. This brings into focus not only the rift in Protestantism but the nature and extent of the crisis in which the Church finds herself at this moment of her history.

In the light of these external and internal crises which the Church faces, there is an urgent need to reexamine our missionary methods. New skills and technological developments have arisen which need to be fully understood and adapted to the demands of the situation. There is also an urgent need to rethink existing methods. The growing tide of nationalism and antiwhite feeling throughout much of the world make a critical reappraisal of missionary strategy essential. This does not imply that all past policies must be scrapped;

3. Lesslie Newbigin, *The Household of God* (New York: Friendship Press, 1954), p. 94.
4. *Ibid.,* p. 95.

but what it does mean is that we must be willing to adapt ourselves, in the best biblical manner, to the situation as it exists. The Old Testament teaches us as many lessons from the defeats of God's armies as it does from their victories. We shall need a spirit of divine humility if we are to learn from recent missionary history. And learn we must. It is imperative that we rethink our attitudes to such thorny problems as ecclesiastical organization, national Christians and younger churches, totalitarian governments, and revolutionary movements.

Our purpose in this book is to mention some of the most obvious and pressing developments that complicate the task of world evangelization. We do not profess to have the answers to all the issues. We do try to make some suggestions. If we are to serve our generation in the will of God, we must know that generation. The first step in this process is to face some disturbing questions. This is the task to which we address ourselves in the pages of this book.

Part I. The Church on the Defensive

Chapter 1: Revolution: Man's Striving for Justice

To many western observers the world is twisted and tottering on the brink of an atomic holocaust. Discordant cries come from every quarter. Headlines continually convey bad news. Established institutions are crumbling on a massive and terrifying, worldwide scale. The savage mutterings of the rough undernourished, comprising the vast majority of the world's population, understandably create fear in the hearts and minds of the privileged few.

In such an hour the committed Christian dare not play the passive role of a spectator. If God is the God of history, and the Christian has been called to be a co-worker, then God's activity in history must be discovered and understood. Without such a continuing search and reappraisal the Christian cannot relate himself to the divine purpose of world evangelization.

We must face the facts—the facts of human frustration, revolution, and social reconstruction. These are

17

among the dominant characteristics of the world today, whether we think of the Far East or the Middle East, New York or New Delhi, Africa or Latin America.

Frustration

Some four hundred years ago Thomas Cranmer, the first Protestant Archbishop of Canterbury, observed: "Food grows dearer. Do our brothers grow dearer too? No—they freeze and starve beneath our heaven-bent feet." Recently the trend reached fruition, at least symbolically, when four hundred years later a priest in Spain watched a shrine burning and said, "The Church forgot the poor—now the poor have forgotten the Church." [1]

During these four hundred years, especially during the last few decades, a profound change has taken place in human affairs. The pent-up frustrations and resentments of the past that have been locked up in the breasts of the exploited, underprivileged masses of mankind have at last reached bursting point. These pressures can no longer be contained by the appeals of the ruling classes that the *status quo* is attributable to God's immutable decrees or the innate superiority of the West. Neither force nor law can restrain them. It is almost trite to say that a new era is dawning and the world will never be the same again. The very people who formerly "did not count" are now manifesting their restlessness

---

1. Milton Mayer, "Christ Under Communism," *Harper's Magazine,* August 1960, p. 30.

and their passion to share in the benefits of Western technology and freedom. Theirs is the largely unfulfilled desire to be themselves, to be respected, to have both prestige and the power to direct their own communal affairs. A new consciousness that people need no longer suffer pointlessly, but can influence, even change, the structure of society, is one of the most influential factors of our time.

This climate of frustration has arisen for three chief reasons. The first reason arises out of the relationship between the "population explosion" and the problem of food. Among the non-white races today there is a rate of population increase unprecedented in human history. The over-all annual increase is almost fifty millions. In the next forty years world population will double, reaching the staggering total of 5.4 billions. Pessimistic Malthus's short essay of almost two centuries ago is being studied with mounting concern. Can food production keep pace with the population increase? [2]

Already in many agrarian countries of the world, the land is thus far able to provide only for the minimum survival requirements of its people. Times of drought, flood, or epidemic are times of acute distress and starvation. True, efforts are being made to improve farming

2. Thomas R. Malthus, *Essay on the Principle of Population*, first published in 1798. His thesis was that population increases more rapidly than food supplies. He argued that there will always be more people in the world than can be fed, and wars and disease are more or less necessary to kill off extra population. Malthus, Huxley, and Osborn, *Three Essays on Population* (Mentor ed.; New York: New American Library of World Literature, Inc., 1960).

methods, but the question remains whether in the future the land will be able to support the enormous increase in people who must live on it. Can sufficient land be cultivated to meet increasing food demands? The 1951 census of India contains the prognosis that the total increase of agricultural productivity possible in India will enable the country to produce, at most, food sufficient for 450 million people—the estimated population for 1969.[3]

Not only in India, but in many parts of the world, food is becoming more scarce and more expensive. A crisis is mounting. Previously, with no prospect or concept of changing centuries-old social structures and patterns of agriculture, the hungry were tempted to despair. But today they are not resigning themselves to their fate. They are restless to break out of the bondage of this frustration.

This introduces the second reason for today's crisis. It is the outcome of the worldwide dissemination of Western thought and ideals, of Western economic and social achievements. These are days in which millions throughout the world, through films, magazines, books, and schools, are coming to realize that in the West— the U.S.A. and Canada, Britain and segments of western Europe, Australia and New Zealand—there is a type of society, an affluent society, in which the age-long problems of hunger, poverty, and disease have

---

3. Quoted by Rajah B. Manikam, *Christianity and the Asian Revolution* (New York: Friendship Press, 1954), p. 29.

been largely resolved. Abundance has become the possession of the many rather than the privilege of the few. It is not fully appreciated at home that the Church has had no small part in precipitating this ferment by means of its missionary outreach. She has brought literacy and education to many parts of the world. She has taught the importance and dignity of the individual. She has planted the seeds not merely of personal and spiritual revolution through Christ, but also of social and economic revolution.

At the same time this ferment has generated bitterness. "Why," these people ask, "should the average American be so wealthy when we are all so poor? Why is it that in our country the wealth is concentrated in the hands of so few? These few were not created congenitally superior to us. Are we not as good as they? Why is it that, while the white, Christian nations ruled over us, they did not make serious efforts to raise the general economic level of our society?" Today the world's awakened peoples are demanding immediate and radical changes in their social systems. They naturally want to enjoy economic "utopia" in their own generation. How impatient they are! And herein lies the crux, for they press their leaders: "We want a change! We want a change to take place now. Don't tell us to wait until tomorrow. If you do, we will find other leaders—the sort that will help us today!"

This appeal points up the third reason for the present worldwide crisis in frustration. Communist achievements and communist literature have convinced the world that it is possible for backward, agrarian nations to transform themselves into first-class industrial powers within a few decades. Their apologists cry out: "Look at the Soviet Union! Forty years ago Russia was a demoralized, backward nation. Today, despite a most devastating war with the Nazis, the Soviet Union is on the way to becoming the most powerful nation in the world. What nation can match its rapid industrial growth? Look at its scientific and athletic achievements, its cultural and military power. The capitalistic West has not helped us. But the Soviet Union will. The Soviets have pledged themselves to save all nations from imperialism, from colonialism, from exploitation, and from poverty. Our own politicians have endlessly pledged land reform, but have not seriously tried to redistribute the land among the people. But you cannot name a communist leader who has failed in this regard! 'Workers of the world unite, you have nothing to lose but your chains!' "

Great restless masses are coming to see the possibility of actively participating in righting an unjust world. Mass education programs, political rallies, the persuasive propaganda of the Communists—all these have made men impatient with the age-long role of passivity and submission to a harsh, oppressive existence. The call is to revolution. It falls on the ears of many, eager to march under any banner and behind any leader. The present system must be swept away. Harold J. Laski, authoritative economist, historian and political scientist, in his book *Reflections on the Revolution of Our Time* summarized our era thus: "We are in the midst of a period of revolutionary change that is likely to be as profound as any in the modern history of the human race."

Revolution

What are the chief characteristics of this era of revolution? First and foremost is the relative decline of the West. The West greatly weakened itself through two disastrous world wars and several minor ones in the earlier decades of this century. Has the West reached the point of no return? Barraclough, a prominent British historian, recently asked the pointed question, "Was the war of 1939–45 the decisive conflict in which Europe committed suicide and surrendered mastery to the colored people?" [4] Many assert that by its protracted internecine wars the West has lost whatever prior claim it may have had to the moral leadership of the world. It has burned itself out. This means that throughout the former colonial countries of Asia and Africa, the communist whispering campaign that "Christianity is a white-man's religion" is having the damaging effect of identifying the message of God's eternal Son, the Light of the world, with a popularly discredited people. Even the West's economic leadership is being challenged by

---

4. Geoffrey Barraclough, *History in a Changing World* (London: Blackwell, 1956), p. 182.

the communist bloc. In Latin America, anti-Western feeling is so strong that in many republics politicians have found it impossible to win a popular election without paying respects to Castro's Cuba or to Moscow. Concomitantly it is political suicide to be overly friendly toward Washington.

Second, this era of revolution is characterized also by the emergence of new countries. Early in the twentieth century, before the West began seriously to consider relinquishing its overseas holdings, independence movements started stirring. With the close of World War II, economic impoverishment at home as well as political considerations pressed the West, not only to consider liquidating foreign holdings, but to accelerate withdrawal from the once fascinating and profitable commerce of imperialism and colonialism. These factors greatly abetted the emergence of many new and independent countries throughout the world. In 1945 almost seven-eighths of all Muslims lived under colonial rule. Since that time, however, almost every Muslim country has gained its independence. In the decade since 1952, no less than twenty-six countries in the continent of Africa alone achieved their independence.

A third characteristic of this era is the new type of political revolution that has become widespread. In the past, revolutions often merely substituted a government drawn from one class for another government formed from the same class. Frequently they were little more than a junta or cabinet reshuffle. Bolivia averaged more than one such revolution per year since gaining her independence in 1825![5] But this type of revolution did not significantly affect the lives of the mass of its citizens. Revolutions today, however, are vastly different. They have a new dimension in their resentment—one of depth. Their objective is not merely to remove a government but irrevocably to repudiate the whole class from which that government was drawn. These revolutions are remarkably similar in important respects to the 1789-style revolution in the classical tradition— a tradition which unfortunately dovetails fairly readily into the communist coup. Once in the saddle, with no previous political experience or prospects, the new elite ruthlessly eliminate or suppress the old ruling classes, along with the privileges they abused. This type of revolution, or modifications of it, is becoming increasingly common. (Examples from the last decade include Castro's Cuba, Nasser's Egypt, and Kassem's Iraq.)

Fourth, this revolutionary era is producing a drastically altered form of government. Even in this, one can detect an emotional reaction against the West. Having lost her clear-cut political supremacy, the West finds the value of her political institutions have become suspect. As the center of world power and influence shifts toward the non-Christian world, national and international forces (generally of a non-Western stamp) have been competing for the allegiance of the new states.

---

5. John C. Thiessen, *A Survey of World Missions* (Chicago: Inter-Varsity Press, 1955), p. 364.

Inevitably, with such competing interests there have been collisions and compromises (e.g., Congo and Laos). In the ensuing flux, communist totalitarianism, religious nationalism (Islamic or Buddhist), several varieties of Asian socialism, Ghandhism, secularized democracy—all have been striving for political power. Although the end is not yet in sight, the drift is toward totalitarianism, the planned economy, the one-leader, one-political-philosophy type of government.

A fifth characteristic of today's revolutionary era is the worldwide socio-economic shift it is producing. For want of a better term, one might say the world is experiencing "international civil war." This is something far more extensive than the East-West struggle. In fact, within both communist and Western spheres of influence, as well as self-styled neutral states, there is economic and social upheaval; sometimes it takes the form of a subdued protest, sometimes violence. But whatever form it takes, it represents a major change in the character of our civilization. Human history has seen many upheavals in the past, but there are startling differences in the crises of today. Technological development and improved communication have greatly accelerated the rate of change and made it worldwide in scope. Previously a Roman Empire could collapse in Europe without disturbing a Chinese or Indian civilization in Asia. But in today's "one world" no nation lives unto itself. Each influences the other; their lives and fortunes are intimately interrelated.

The character of this socio-economic revolution, or at least its bases, need to be examined carefully. After centuries characterized by village-centered, raw-material-producing (sometimes mere subsistence-farming) agricultural societies deeply subservient to feudalistic overlords, the industrial revolution has suddenly and violently descended upon these countries. Their leaders are convinced that industrialization is essential to survival. Undoubtedly this is an entirely accurate assessment—but in the meantime many agrarian societies are experiencing stress and anguish over their efforts to create, in the shortest possible time, industrial complexes that took the West many decades to erect. Crowded, ugly cities are mushrooming everywhere—cities filled with restless crowds in revolt against poverty, and struggling to build a Western-type industrial system while striving to achieve economic and cultural independence of the West.

Typically the new city dwellers are restless. Many were formerly farmers. Their heritage was one of oppression and want. They and their forebears were the ones who earnestly debated the ancient and crucial problem: "Who shall own the land?" For centuries millions of peasant families owned small plots of land, but never enough to live on. Additional land had to be rented from the landlord and worked for him for an agreed percentage of the crop. The landlord, in order to insure a satisfactory income, would stimulate peasants to bid among themselves for the opportunity of cul-

27

tivating his land. A tenant who delivered sixty per cent of the crop might be evicted if another offered to deliver seventy per cent. If any tenant fell behind in his deliveries, he would have to mortgage his own land to the landlord. This would sometimes result in the landlord's being tempted to foreclose on the mortgage, thereby adding to his land holdings. This often happened. In past centuries the landlord's abuses were tempered by the threat of peasant uprisings, but in the twentieth century the landowner's hold has been generally strengthened by Western influences and sometimes also by a more centralized system of government capable of suppressing armed intimidation.

It can easily be seen that land reform offers an irresistible attraction to the peasant. He readily gives his loyalty to the political movement, regardless of its position on personal freedom, that pledges to deliver him from the landlord's deadly grip. Throughout Asia, Africa, and Latin America, in every political rally, in every election campaign, one encounters variations of the slogan: "Those owning the land must work the land." "Down with Absentee-Landlordism." The peasant will invariably turn against any form of government that allows itself to be controlled by landlords. This was the reason why the post World War II peasant armies of Chiang Kai-shek refused to oppose the Communists. They realized that he would not face the issue that his party had become landlord-dominated. They repudi-

28

ated his leadership and welcomed the Communists as liberators.

One can affirm without qualification that the government of every new nation today is threatened more by communist success in industrializing backward nations, and thereby solving the problem of the peasant and his poverty, his land and livelihood, than by the appeal of Marxian political philosophy as distinct from its economic aspects. Today all Asian eyes are fixed on China and all Latin American eyes on Cuba. Will they succeed? If they do, and if non-communist India fails to solve this problem, nothing will stand in the way of the triumph of the Communists throughout much of the world.

To summarize very simply: the world is in revolutionary upheaval. Leaders are acutely aware of population trends, limited food supplies, the growing restlessness of the displaced farmers forming the new urban masses. These leaders continue to appeal to large nations, East and West, for economic aid. Their peoples must be settled and satisfied. Work and food must be provided. Industrialization and scientific farming must be introduced on a massive scale if there is to be any hope of future survival.

Christian Participation

What is to be the role of the Christian in this world of revolution? Foremost, he must learn to live with revo-

29

lution, for this is the climate of the age. But what do we mean by this?

Some Christians affirm that their task is to concentrate on church matters and avoid dealing with what they term the "economic grievances and animal appetites" of man. They desire to live with revolution as one lives with the remembrance of a bad dream. Theirs is the posture of withdrawal, an escape into pietism or science or art. They say: "We must preserve our faith. We must keep ourselves free from corruption, especially from political corruption. All world systems are evil. Unless you withdraw from them you cannot attain holiness." And yet, the Christian can no more successfully withdraw from the political questions of his day than a fish can withdraw from the water in which it lives. In fact, any form of escapism is but a tacit political vote for the *status quo,* possibly a vote for the reactionary.

Other Christians cling to Romans 13:1–2 to defend the *status quo,* regardless of its immorality and injustice. ". . . the governing authorities . . . have been instituted by God. Therefore he who resists the authorities resists what God has appointed, and those who resist will incur judgment." But is the matter as simple as this? If a country has had three revolutions in one year (this has happened!), which of the three governments should the Christian recognize, and at what stage in the struggle does he change his allegiance from one to the other? To what authority should the Chinese Christian look—Peking or Taipei? One third of the world is under a communist rule that is avowedly atheistic. Where can they draw the line between loyalty to God and loyalty to Caesar?

Indifference to political questions is a sin. One's Christian integrity demands dangerous political choices. To be non-participating and/or merely fatalistic is to be unbelieving. Certainly, Scripture always points the Christian to the way of faith, with the implication that God is at work in society today and that participation with Him is possible.

But this participation with Him is not going to be easy. In the long years of its evolution, Protestantism has become a comfortable middle-class movement. Since it is bound to lose this preferential position if there is any drastic revolutionary change in the pattern of society, it has allowed itself to become imprisoned in the camp of political conservatism. With the shift toward the anonymity of modern mass society, it has increasingly lost contact with the oppressed, the frustrated, the rebellious. It is therefore not surprising to discover that most independence or revolutionary movements in the world today have taken an anti-Christian position at their inception.

There has been a notable exception to this trend. Reference is to the deep interest of Christians in the social evolution of Great Britain. Referring to this, Stephen Neill has commented:

It was this Christian leaven in the working class, together with the Christian Socialist movement of

31

F. D. Maurice, Charles Kingsley and their friends, that gave to the British Labour movement up to the end of the nineteenth century a character so different from that of similar movements in other countries. Throughout the nineteenth century all over the continent of Europe it was taken for granted that the church would always be on the side of power against the oppressed, and that it would resolutely oppose any change in the *status quo*. It is only in this century that Christians on the continent have found it possible to take their place naturally within the parties of the left; and the separation between church and working class became far more radical than it ever was in Britain.[6]

One need not be a theologian to detect that the God of the Old Testament is a God who is passionately concerned about personal ethics and social justice. Some evangelicals have rationalized away the timeless significance of the longings of the Psalmists and denunciations of the Prophets. They have concluded that God turned off His attribute of concern for social justice with the Day of Pentecost. They are almost vehement in their affirmations that He doesn't care today whether people are hungry or living a debased existence. He is only interested in getting them saved and heavenbound. He is indifferent to the oppression and injustice that stalk abroad in the earth. At His Second Coming, however, He will reactivate His attribute of social

6. Stephen Neill, *The Unfinished Task*. (London: Lutterworth Press, 1957), p. 76.

concern. Then "righteousness shall reign" on the earth. This is a seriously defective and distorted image of God's true nature and concern. He is as burdened about social justice today as He ever was in Amos's day.

The responsible Christian who cannot ignore his own political existence rejoices in the opportunity in this area to be venturesome for his Lord. He is determined to break with the mentality that is a succession of negatives: anti-Communist, anti-alcohol, anti-change, anti-theater, anti-tobacco—"Christianity gone cultic." Furthermore, he recognizes that political ideologies infiltrate the entire realm of society and its culture, often laying claim to providing total explanations for human existence. They all too frequently demand a total dedication that is idolatrous. In such a field it is not always easy to face up to the fact that political action is rarely possible without some form of compromise. The method of the group is not always on the same ethical level as the method of the individual.

But in spite of the difficulties, the earnest Christian is not willing to deceive himself with the illusion that being neutral is being moral. He knows that to refuse to act politically is frequently in itself a political act— the rubber stamping of social injustice or irresponsibility in international affairs. Evangelicals were among those who withheld support from Woodrow Wilson in his efforts to found a strong League of Nations. The subsequent failure of the League, in the absence of the United States, contributed to the rise of nazism. In

33

Germany the evangelical community failed to offer any significant protest until some time after Hitler assumed the chancellorship. Recent history is replete with the tragedies that have resulted from the political irresponsibility of Christians who gloried in their neutralism.

It is often observed that our evangelistic efforts are geared for the disillusioned and defeated. We reach out almost exclusively to the man flat on his back, so to speak, and leave that man running headlong toward the precipice without so much as a sympathetic word of warning. Perhaps this is because it is easier to say "I told you so" than to love my neighbor as myself. We seem, at least temporarily, unequal to the task of winning those who are caught up in the excitement and hope of a world in revolution. All we do is to labor out at the fringes, recruiting the isolated strays, those out of step with the times.

These judgments contain elements of both truth and error. It is true that every segment of society needs to be reached and won. But equally valid is the fact that ultimately all political movements, despite their enthusiasm and devotion, lead to disillusionment. Unaided man cannot perfect human society. This does not mean, however, that the Christian should stand on the sidelines, waiting for the inevitable corrosion to set in, and then begin his evangelism with an I-told-you-so approach. Such a posture makes Christianity appear to be unworthy of survival.

Christians need to catch the mood of the times. This was vividly described by Leon M. Guerrero, the Philippine Ambassador in London, in a speech delivered in Britain.

> In most of Asia, . . . the crust of ancient custom still remains. But it is only a crust, and what is underneath is very new . . . ancient Asia is reborn. . . . she is young again, she is full of hope. She is everything that the young are: enthusiastic, quarrelsome, idealistic, impulsive, intolerant, generous in sacrifice, sanguine in expectations, and often divided in heart and divided in purpose. . . .
>
> To the traveler from Asia, Europe seems old and weary, tired of so much history, tired of making it and enduring it. . . . Europe just wants to be left alone. But young Asia has a lot of history before her; she wants to get so many things done that the past left undone. In terms of history, it is the Asians who are the new Elizabethans, sure of honor and glory, reckless of the odds, enchanted by self-discovery, feverishly impatient of success.
>
> . . . All [Asians] . . . are engaged in the same task, each in their own chosen spirit, with their own approach and methods: and we are all reorganizing the structure of society . . . we all have our five-year, seven-year, ten-year programs.[7]

Recognizing that the Church's intransigence in the revolutionary ferment of today may spell its doom, the responsible Christian seeks to participate in the press-

7. L. M. Guerrero, *Alternatives for Asians: The Philippine Experiment* (London: The Philippine Embassy, 1957), p. 10.

ing task of relieving human misery and fighting alongside others for a better tomorrow. He participates as a learner, confessing his past social indifference and isolationism while seeking to contribute his best. He is not using his own participation as a front for a Christian apologia, but is genuinely concerned with the political issues at stake. However, neither does he betray Christ by hiding His person nor forget the absolute Kingdom He will eventually establish for the human family.

The Christian recognizes that order in society comes from God (Romans 13:1–7; I Timothy 2:1–2). God is deeply concerned with maintaining peace and justice. Since, under God's ordination, voting power is granted to every citizen, the Christian who fails to vote is unfaithful to his God. So long as the social structure can be altered by peaceful means, it is the Christian's political responsibility to do all he can to remove abuses and ameliorate inequalities. He does this by personal investigation, participation in political discussions, and use of the ballot box.

When the pattern is not democratic and the privilege of suffrage is not granted, the Christian is still responsible to love his neighbor as himself (Matthew 25:31–40). The Lord of the poor, the Lord of the oppressed, the Lord of the imprisoned, still demands his political activity. How could it be otherwise? There can be no dodging even the most controversial issues. To love one's neighbor means to concern oneself with his need for bread, clothing, shelter, economic security, peace, education, and freedom, as well as his fundamental need for Jesus Christ. To express this love may sometimes involve one in great personal danger. Some Christians in the West may be appalled to learn that a number of Christian students were killed in the riots that brought down the corrupt government of Syngman Rhee in Korea in 1960. It is probable that these students felt that the only way they could love their neighbor practically was to involve themselves in the dangerous business of seeking to pull down a government that did not really have the best interests of the people at heart. And they were killed, seeking to do what they felt to be the will of God.

Abraham Lincoln, a man of peace and Christian conviction, while a congressman (1848), challenged President Polk's Mexican war policy by making a clear-cut affirmation about the right of revolution. He said, "Any people anywhere, being inclined and having the power, have the right to rise up and shake off the existing government, and form a new one that suits them better. This is a most valuable, a most sacred right—a right which we hope and believe is to liberate the world." Christians living in today's world need to take far more seriously than they do their God-given obligations to concern themselves with the total need of their fellow men. They must speak up and act as responsible moral beings in the immoral society in which God has placed them.

"Educated men become Communists chiefly for moral

37

reasons," [8] is the affirmation of Whittaker Chambers. This judgment is confirmed by the book, *The God that Failed*, containing the testimonies of six prominent men of letters in the Western world whose involvement, and subsequent disillusionment, with the Communist Party arose because of indignation against injustice either in their own experience or in the society of which they were members. All six felt the Church's posture toward society to be completely irrelevant, because of the failure of its members to display any genuine social concern. The Church can no longer enjoy the luxury of social irresponsibility; she must learn to live with revolution.

The Church today must learn compassion and service, even though it realizes the only lasting hope for society is the return of Christ. It must learn sympathy, even sympathy for the most fanatic Communist as he agitates in a ruthlessly amoral fashion for the impossible ideal of a classless, utopian society. "Please understand, you Christians," one Communist reportedly said, "that for us the situation is far more tragic than for you. We know nothing except history. If you fail you still have your hope in another world. If we fail, we are left with empty hands and without hope." [9]

8. Whittaker Chambers, *Witness* (New York: Random House, 1952), p. 8.

9. Philippe Maury, *Politics and Evangelism* (Garden City: Doubleday, 1959), p. 99.

Chapter 2: **Nationalism: The Hunger for Relevance**

Nationalism is the great, profoundly elemental force in human affairs today. It should be appreciated, but must also be feared. It may indicate progress, but can also herald the coming of Antichrist.

Opinions concerning nationalism are sharply divided. On one hand, for example, a missionary working in the Congo pleads for our fellowship in praying away this menace. On the other hand, speaking at a recent missionary convention for university students with great eloquence and enthusiasm, an African exchange student heralds the rising tide of nationalism in Africa today as the will of God. Apparently with official consent, the senior program of a prominent Bible school includes the statement that colonial leaders approve missions because they have "helped to subdue the nationalist spirit of the people of Africa." In contrast, one of our popular evangelical magazines reports a responsible Protestant leader's defence of nationalism as inevitable, even desirable.

Plainly, nationalism is a controversial issue. Some scholars would go so far as to state that in the totality of human history, it is a phenomenon peculiar to the twentieth century.[1] Since the Christians living in this generation are primarily responsible for evangelizing the peoples of this generation, they must give serious and thorough study to nationalism now. They cannot—they dare not—overlook it. The Christian who faces the fact of his missionary responsibility will encounter this problem head-on, whether he labors in Japan or Kenya, in Latin America or Southeast Asia.

What Is Nationalism?

Just what is this compelling loyalty we term nationalism? In the world today three major types have been distinguished.[2]

1. Self-expressive nationalism

This is the nationalism of the former colonial world, the form prominent in the news today. It represents the hungerings of many formerly subjugated peoples for self-expression and self-determination. Their drive for independence must not be regarded as a heightened

1. This judgment by Boyd C. Shafer can be found in his significant work, *Nationalism: Myth and Reality* (New York: Harcourt, Brace and Company, 1955), p. 5.

2. This classification is widely used. *The World Mission of the Church* (New York: International Missionary Council, 1939).

patriotism. Those who have seen this type at first-hand, and have felt its pulse, have described it in far stronger language. One such witness has stated, "It is the passion of a people for self-determination, developed to the point of absurdity." Perhaps this definition lacks sympathy. The fact remains that many peoples are awakening to an awareness of themselves. They desire to express themselves, achieve self-respect in the totality of their lives, and determine their own destinies. Christians cannot but be sympathetic with them. We may safely assume that God desires all races and cultures to be free from external domination.

2. Self-satisfied nationalism

This is the nationalism of the West—self-satisfied, contented, smug. Although the long-established nations of Western Europe and North America might loftily describe their national loyalties as patriotism, closer scrutiny will uncover that each country has deeply ingrained in its national consciousness all the basic elements of a full-fledged nationalism. No nation today has a group consciousness that is merely mild patriotism, consonant with biblical principles, and free from racial pride and a sense of cultural superiority.

3. Self-assertive nationalism

This is the nationalism of the Soviet Union and China, though it is not confined to these emerging communist world powers. True, the theoretically correct

41

Communist is an internationalist, who regards all forms of group loyalty as bourgeois. Yet the fact remains that communist practice in the world today is shot through with the contradiction of nationalistic motivations. Marxist Yugoslavia broke with Moscow because its nationalistic feelings were offended by Russian heavy-handedness. This fiercely self-assertive type of nationalism is not unlike the aggressive nationalism of the fascist powers of World War II.

Even from such a brief survey as this we find that nationalism is not static, but dynamic. Self-expressive nationalism can become self-satisfied or self-assertive from a great variety of causes. In fact, the tendency toward change is inherent in the sheer irrationality of nationalism. Nationalism—regardless of type—is a smouldering vision in the minds of men, a fire burning in their bones, a yearning, a cluster of convictions deep within their hearts that defies precise and acceptable definition.[3] It is not necessarily related either to facts or reason. As a result, it always poses grave problems even to its leaders, as they seek to direct its impulsive drives into constructive, orderly channels.

How might a mild self-expressive nationalism develop into the aggressive type? Remembering that na-

---

3. M. A. C. Warren, in his article "Nationalism as an International Asset," defines nationalism in its broadest sense as "the self-conscious assertion by a people of its own individuality in relation to other peoples." *The International Review of Missions*, XLIV (October, 1955), 387.

tionalism is a mysterious compound of a variety of components, let us begin with the soil. Nationalism starts with a love for a unit of territory, coveted or possessed. This love is harnessed to a desire for political independence, i.e., for self-expression. In many emerging nations today, this yearning is enveloped in a mysterious, idolatrous devotion to the tribe or nation which in its own public mind has become something greater than the mere aggregate of its parts. Its protagonists call for loyalty, for devotion, for solidarity. Soon the dogma emerges that personal significance is discovered only as a man lives for the group. This tends to lead to a sense of group superiority. The conviction grows that the nation does not need to identify itself with other nations, or with any religion other than that which is indigenous to the group, in order to attain its true significance. It asserts *itself*. It soon feels that it is unique, even superior to other cultures. At this point nationalism can turn either to the right and become self-satisfied, or veer to the left and become aggressive. "By inherent qualifications and right we should be supreme among the nations"—this is the cry. Although the self-satisfied nationalism of the West today may be static and defensive, its alternative—the self-aggressive type—may reach the point of no return and precipitate aggressive wars. The last few decades loudly warn us against underestimating the nihilistic nature of nationalism. The records of Italian fascism, German nazism, and Japanese Shintoism all speak for themselves. This form of nationalism is ever blindly contemptuous of the rights of smaller, weaker nations.

This then is nationalism—as Toynbee defines it, "the worship of collective human power within local limits." [4] Despite its myths and actualities, its truths and errors, it is a contemporary phenomenon of incalculable emotional force.

Nationalism in Today's World

How and where did nationalism originate? There are those who would say that the world is in social revolution chiefly because of the ideas that have been disseminated by the Western imperialist nations through their economic exploitation, the work of their missionaries, and the evidence of Western superiority in material culture manifest around the globe.

Such ideas and impressions gained from the West have awakened the underprivileged peoples from the torpor of their past. They have gradually become aware of themselves and their exploitation by the white man. Previously they had largely accepted misery, poverty, ignorance, and disease as their lot—the same tragic circumstances their parents and grandparents experienced before them. But they have now come to realize that the white races, whom they have found to be no better than themselves, have largely solved these problems in

---

4. Arnold J. Toynbee, *Christianity Among the Religions of the World* (New York: Charles Scribner's Sons, 1957), pp. 14, 15, 53.

their home countries. Why should they continue to be exploited so that these foreigners can be made more comfortable? Why not throw overboard the role of cultural inferiority unconsciously assumed in earlier decades? Why not get rid of the white man while at the same time adopting some of his advantages? Why not be free to use the resources of one's own country to benefit one's own people?

While the above may satisfy as a general explanation for the emergence of nationalism, the evangelical Christian should view the problem in the larger context of contemporary world events. What is the major thrust of the worldwide crisis of our times? In describing the current international situation, Toynbee has emphatically stated:

> I believe it is a foregone conclusion that the world is going to be unified politically in the near future. . . . I think the big and really formidable political issue today is, not whether the world is soon going to be unified politically, but in which of two alternative possible ways this rapid unification is going to come about.[5]

It is in this context of the rapid movement toward worldwide political unification that we should approach the localized phenomenon of nationalism, for there are those who argue that the very presence of nationalism

---

5. Arnold J. Toynbee, *Civilization on Trial* (New York: Oxford University Press, 1948), p. 127.

is an indication that the world's drift is toward political unity under some form of world government.

This may seem contradictory. Is not nationalism the deadly foe of internationalism? Do not nationalist movements represent the desires of peoples, long subjugated, to have their own separate existence? Do they not represent progress in the best sense of the term, in that the once subjugated and exploited are becoming increasingly free to express their own distinctive national cultures?

There is another aspect, however, to the emergence of these nationalistic movements. The self-expressive type of nationalism, by its very tendency to drift toward aggressiveness, is an expression of a sense of inferiority and insecurity. This aggressiveness in turn leads ambitious leaders to exploit people's fears to create national blocs along either historical and/or racial lines—e.g., the Pan-Arab and Pan-African movements. It represents the struggles of minority cultures and races to maintain their separateness and distinctiveness in a world that is moving toward cultural unity and the deculturalized anonymity of modern mass society. These minority groups have been endlessly buffeted down through the years, and as the pawns of powerful states they have experienced an accumulation of frustration. Would they never become free in order to "be themselves"? With the breakdown of the colonial empires following World War II, the underprivileged saw their opportunity. The time had come for them to strike out for a separate existence. Their desire to succeed was exceeded only by their determination to survive in a world torn by the titanic struggles of the massive power blocs. As minority groups they withdrew into themselves, seeking to return, metaphorically speaking, to the security and shelter of the womb of their ancient tribal life and religion, real or idealized. Because of the dynamic quality of nationalism, it may eventually manifest a tendency to pervert itself by giving itself up to the idolatrous worship of the newborn nation-states. A person's nationalism then becomes his religion.

The religious aspects of nationalism become increasingly more apparent with the passage of time. Nationalism appears to meet certain fundamental needs of man: his desire for purpose in life, his need for individual significance, and his craving for security. Its evangelists cry: "Save our national community. You belong to us, we belong to you. We are racially and culturally superior to others. Let us face the crises of our day together. We have survived upheavals in the past; we shall do so again." These basic hungerings in a man's heart become especially insistent at a time of upheaval such as the world is experiencing today. Certainly in its religious aspect, this is something with which Christians should have nothing to do. The Church should stand in judgment on the idolatrous worship of man. We should affirm that God and God alone should be worshipped.

All this is of tremendous significance to the evangelical Christian. The biblical revelation of the climax of human history predicts present-day trends in nationalism. Christ himself predicted the latter-day resurgence of Israel and the Gentile nations.[6] More recently, Toynbee has spoken of future world government. The Bible states that before the final Day of God there will emerge on earth a final expression of mankind's agelong apostasy, Antichrist's kingdom. Nationalism simply heralds the dawn of man's world government and its worship of collective man on a worldwide scale. The increasing emergence of nationalism is but an ominous indication of the lateness of the hour. Its presence should challenge Christians, as never before, to accelerate the great task of completing the Church through the evangelization of the world.

The Christian's Great Temptation

Nationalism must also be seen for what it truly is—a potentially mortal enemy. Christ has all too often been made the parasite of nationalism. Any careful student of history can demonstrate this by citing numerous illustrations of the disasters that Christians have courted and embraced down through the years, whenever they have poured their strength and resources into furthering the political ambitions of their own countries.

To illustrate, here is a recent description of Martin Luther and his influence on German Protestants even in the twentieth century.

6. "The fig tree, and all the trees" (Luke 21:29–33).

The great founder of Protestantism was both a passionate anti-Semite and a ferocious believer in absolute obedience to political authority. He wanted Germany rid of the Jews and when they were sent away he advised that they be deprived of "all their cash and jewels and silver and gold" and, furthermore, "that their synagogues or schools be set on fire, that their houses be broken up and destroyed . . . and they be put under a roof or stable, like the gypsies . . . in misery and captivity as they incessantly lament and complain to God about us"—advice that was literally followed four centuries later by Hitler, Goering and Himmler.

. . . .

The influence of this towering figure extended down the generations in Germany, especially among the Protestants. Among other results was the ease with which German Protestantism became the instrument of royal and princely absolutism from the sixteenth century until the kings and princes were overthrown in 1918. . . . In no country with the exception of Czarist Russia did the clergy become by tradition so completely servile to the political authority of the State. . . . Like Niemoeller, most of the pastors welcomed the advent of Adolf Hitler to the chancellorship in 1933.[7]

In the past, Christians have all too often carelessly identified Christ with their Caesars. Today if Christians are not extremely careful in this regard, if they

---

7. William L. Shirer, *The Rise and Fall of the Third Reich* (New York: Simon and Schuster, 1960), pp. 236–237. Copyright © 1960 by the author. Quoted by permission of the publisher.

unconsciously or deliberately equate the political programs of their own countries with God's will, it can well mean that our day may mark the rapid disappearance of biblical Christianity.

Why such a categorical statement? Two reasons suggest themselves.

First, one must not lose sight of the dynamic quality of the Communists' world crusade. Their propaganda is powerful and persuasive, since they constantly hammer on the line that the Church is the captive and agent of "capitalist imperialism." A ground swell of suspicion and hostility toward the Church is rising throughout the world.

Secondly, there is the fact of God and His moral judgments. If there is no self-examination, no self-judgment on the part of His people when they allow His Name and Church to be defiled by alliances with the naked self-interest of the state, how can one count on God's continued patience? In fact, deterioration has already set in. We need to keep in mind the experience of the Roman Catholic Church in Italy. Its blindness today is a reflection of its past. Recall the way it tolerated and even agreed with Mussolini's boastful patriotism. On one occasion he stated before the Roman Senate: "Just think what our Italy has done for the wretched little Oriental sect that started life far away in Palestine where it had no prospect or no influential members. Left to itself Christianity would have been bound to wither and die away. It was salvaged, thanks to being carried to Rome. There the Italian genius made its [the Church's] fortune. And now it has become the universal Roman Catholic Church of which Italy has the honor to be the center." [8] The Vatican's only reaction was to publicly slap Mussolini's wrist, but it nonetheless made a concordat with him in order to gain control of the Italian public school system. Both Mussolini and the Vatican, however, suffered through this union. It is not accidental that the largest communist party in western Europe today is in Italy.

But the Protestants, too, have courted trouble through identifying themselves and their churches with political programs. One has only to recall the Huguenot movement, pre-war Protestantism in Japan, and the many other tragic examples of unscriptural unions between church and state with which history is replete. Never has it been more necessary to separate these two than today, when nationalism is such a powerful force throughout the earth. For example, why is the organized Protestant church in China today so close to extinction as a vital, spiritual force? It was too slow in coming to grips with this peril. Many of its members failed to recognize and deal with elements of uncrucified nationalism within their own hearts. They made peace with their government too early. Not only were they uncritical of its policies, but more often than not they praised its activities, even when it deliberately sought

---

8. Toynbee, *Civilization on Trial*, p. 94.

to inject a divisive spirit into their congregations, stirring up discord among Christians through the organization of accusation meetings. Too often Christians tolerated and were loyal to this arrogantly atheistic state. Thus, slowly, a cancer set in which ate its way into the very vitals of church life. Moral sensibilities were weakened through protracted compromise. When many of our Chinese brethren began to awaken to the realization that they had rendered too much to Caesar and too little to God, their churches had already been penetrated and defiled.

The Foe of Christian Internationalism

All that we have considered so far, and most of what we see of nationalist movements in the world today, would appear to confirm the thesis that nationalism is incompatible with the Christian faith. This does not mean that the right of peoples to self-determination, to their own national life is invalid. The Christian does not condone, much less approve, the view that powerful nations have the right to conquer and subjugate less powerful nations. Where nationalism is but the self-conscious assertion of a people of their own corporateness, it may be conceded as biblically sound. God loves both nations and peoples as such. In Isaiah 19:24–25 He speaks of "Egypt my people, and Assyria the work of my hands, and Israel my heritage." The foregoing gives some idea of the balance which Christians should hold and for which they should pray in the realm of nationalism. In the millennial kingdom the glory of the nations, separate and distinct, is brought into Messiah's Zion.

In the present age nationalism with idolatrous overtones is often the unconfessed sin of God's people. If the evangelical Christian believes that he is a member of the Body of Christ and has been joined to each Christian throughout the earth, he should recognize that the Christian Church is a supranational organism, and every Christian needs every other Christian. Each is interdependent. No Christian can afford to be permanently isolated from his fellow Christians. If there is one Head and only one Body, then Christians should seek to enter into one common life, a life that extends around the globe. In the light of this scriptural teaching it would be difficult to absolve any Christian capitulating to the spirit of nationalism. It would be a flagrant contradiction of his position in Christ and within the Church.

It does not follow automatically, however, that Christian churches should shed their national distinctiveness. The new birth makes possible the inward transformation, not loss, of one's personality by the indwelling Holy Spirit. In like manner it is possible for national churches to have their national characteristics divinely transformed. The millennial ideal can be realized, at least in measure, during this Church age.

Nationalism and Missionary Strategy

What should be our missionary strategy in the face of nationalism? Several lines of action suggest themselves.

1. *Identification.* Missionaries are first and chiefly responsible to deal with all elements of nationalism lurking within their own hearts, their sense of superiority, their tendency to critical attitudes toward those of other races and cultures. But they should not stop here. They are also responsible to instruct and warn their fellow-Christians, at home and abroad, concerning the distinctive aspects of nationalism. Scripture clearly speaks of the relationship between the Christian and the civil authority, of the dangers inherent in nationalism, and of the privilege of forsaking and denying one's national origins for the sake of the Gospel. The spirit of uncrucified nationalism is reflected in the words of the popular Japanese Christian writer, Kanzo Uchimura, who said, "I love two J's and no third; one is Jesus and the other is Japan. I do not know which I love more, Jesus or Japan." [9] It may or may not be significant that the Japanese church has yet to experience revival blessing. No church at home or abroad can secure God's favor if it persists in rendering to Caesar the things that are God's alone.

---

9. John M. L. Young, *The Two Empires in Japan* (Tokyo, Japan: The Bible Times Press, 1958), p. 48.

2. *Organization*. The structure of the missionary team is most apropos to the problem of nationalism. The more interracial its composition and leadership and the more international its character, the better it will reflect the supranational quality of the Christian church, whose citizenship is in heaven. A bulletin of the Church Missionary Society from Malaya reported, "It is no accident that in CMS work in Malaya no factor has been more important for breaking down barriers and leading to the first beginnings of a Christian community in some of them, than the fact that the teams consisted of Chinese and Westerners who were able to say 'we' in a fashion that was quite unmistakable." [10]

3. *Methodology*. Indigenous principles are fast becoming the norm rather than the ideal standard. The old paternalism, the "handout" approach of the nineteenth century, must be completely repudiated. Today every national group wants to be itself, independent of all other nations and especially independent of the West. We should respect this. A missionary in the Philippines was approached by a local congregation for funds to build a church. He replied, "If I give you the money, you will have to say, 'This is the building which the Americans gave us.' If you build it yourself, you will be able to say, 'This is the building the Lord gave us.'" They built their own church and became the stronger for doing so.

10. M. A. C. Warren, *C.M.S. Newsletter*, No. 179, January, 1956.

4. *Outreach.* Missionary methodology must go beyond the triad of evangelism, training, and church-planting. Since every race and people has a contribution to make to the glory of God, each national church should have its own missionary outreach. Every national church should be challenged to cross cultural boundaries for the Lord's sake and engage in foreign missionary work. Each local church should be given instruction and an opportunity to express its missionary obedience by sending and supporting its own ambassadors. Such a policy is bound to enrich the total family of God.

Today's world, by its very nationalism, has developed the climate for making possible the completion of God's great worldwide missionary purpose. Already Korean Christians are laboring in Thailand, Japanese evangelists are preaching in Okinawa, and Filipino teachers are going to Indonesia. All these are but straws in the wind. And, thank God, it is a good wind!

Chapter 3: **Communism and Missions**

THE GOSPEL must first be published among all nations." [1] With this forthright, unambiguous statement Christ described the basic condition His Church must fulfill before He returns to consummate the present age. He went on to state that with His coming "in clouds with great power and glory" He will "gather His elect from the . . . ends of the earth. . . ." [2] This event can only take place after the Church has been gathered out of the nations, through the worldwide proclamation of the gospel.

The twentieth century is unique in the history of the Church. In spite of all the weaknesses of organized Christianity, the Church's goal is finally attainable. It is not that vast masses of people are coming to Christ throughout the world, but rather that the gospel is being proclaimed in almost every land, and increasingly among almost every people.

1. Mark 13:10.
2. Mark 13:26, 27.

The Communists Arrive on the Scene

In recent years, however, the Church throughout the world has become painfully aware of a savage competitor. Opposing the followers of Jesus Christ are the disciples of Karl Marx, integrated into the worldwide communist crusade he launched more than a hundred years ago. Within the last four decades this adversary has gained control of roughly one-third the world's population and one-fourth its land surface.

Never before have Christian missionaries faced so baffling, so formidable an opponent. Wherever the Communists have gained political control, aggressive gospel outreach has been first throttled and later forbidden.

Perhaps this is why Pastor Günther Jacob of Cottbus, East Germany, recently raised the question: "Is this the end of the Constantinian era?" [3] He had been analyzing the unrelenting, steadily increasing pressure of the Communists on his parish church. Its corporate life was being hindered, its message assailed as irrelevant, its evangelistic outreach virtually terminated. Economic and social sanctions were being placed upon its membership with a growing official impatience that did not augur well for the future. And this in the very part of Germany intimately associated with Luther and the Reformation!

---

3. Karl Barth and Johannes Hamel, *How to Serve God in a Marxist Land* (New York: Association Press, 1959), p. 64.

What did Pastor Jacob mean by his phrase, "the Constantinian era"? Soon after the conversion of the Emperor Constantine, in 312 A.D., Christianity was made the official religion of the Roman Empire. Almost overnight the church gained a privileged and powerful position in the social structure of the Western world. It has maintained this position until our own generation. A new era is dawning with the advent of communism as a world force. The church is now being pushed rudely back to its pre-Constantinian status, when it was an almost universally despised, frequently persecuted, and (since it was always "out of step" with the *status quo*) seldom ignored movement in society.

Undoubtedly we can affirm that Satan moves behind the vigorous growth of communism in our world. When we realize that his doom is sealed with the return of Christ, then we can expect him to do all within his power to prevent the completion of the worldwide witness of the Church. Today Satan is using communism as he has used no other force in the past to hinder missionary advance. The emergence of communism should be viewed by the Christian as an integral part of Satan's cosmic conflict with Christ.

Reacting Negatively to the Communist Problem

What form should evangelical missionary strategy take in the face of communist advance? Some training schools in America (by their curricula) and some mis-

59

sionaries overseas (by their silence) appear to be quite indifferent to the problem. They seem unaware of communism's dynamic force and awesome magnitude. Indifference born of ignorance appears to insulate many Christians from the realization that communism may well be the pivotal problem facing missionary strategists today.

Others are possibly indifferent because they have unwittingly allowed eschatological views to distort their perspective on their Christian responsibilities. They reason: "Let's face it. We're in the end of the age. Christ's return is imminent. God's people are soon to be delivered out of the mess. Missions? Oh, every age has ended with the failure of God's people. The Church in this age will fail too. Communism? A definite sign of the end. There is little you can do to cope realistically with this early evidence of Antichrist's kingdom."

Reacting Unscripturally to the Communist Problem

The Devil is a master of camouflage. He is also skilled in enticing Christians away from biblical approaches to the problems before them. Nowhere is this more clearly revealed than in the host of nonbiblical approaches to the communist problem into which he has tangled Christians. Some have been trapped into assuming a posture of total, unrelieved hostility toward all Communists. This has made them incapable of winning them to Christ. Others have been tempted to yield theological ground in their efforts to establish rapport with

Communists. This response has merely earned their scorn. Communists rarely yield in matters of ideology, although their capacity for tactical changes is prodigious.

Still others, upon discovering that Communists preach a program of social and political reorganization, have felt that they should compete with a parallel program incorporating religious overtones. In their preoccupation with social and political reform, they have forgotten the primary ministry of reconciliation committed to them by God, a ministry that centers upon preaching the redemptive work of Christ and His cross.

Many have felt that they should identify the Church with the political program of the West in its cold war with the communist powers. This position has been completely misunderstood by nationals overseas. The fact remains that the West, by its very evident prosperity and unsavory past, is more often than not the object of jealousy, suspicion, and even hatred by those whom it once described as "lesser breeds without the law." These uncommitted millions will not be drawn to a Savior whom they regard· as a tool of the imperialist West. The Church cannot fulfill its missionary obligation if it insists on identifying itself with any particular political position or economic philosophy.

Thinking Positively and Scripturally

The thoughtful Christian, believing that God is in command of history, finds it impossible to be indifferent to trends among the nations today. He is confronted with a world that is undergoing a major shift in the balance of power between nations and civilizations. While the white races are in relative political decline, the non-white races are emerging from a formerly passive to an increasingly dominant role on an unprecedented scale. This generation, threatened as it is by communism, must be evangelized. What God commands He also enables us, by His grace, to fulfill. We dare not allow missionary strategy to be crystallized into a holding operation, merely "looking for" the return of Christ. This ultimate triumph can and must be aided by a venturesome application of scriptural principles to the harrowing present. What if Christ delays His return another ten years—or a hundred? Aimless "muddling along" will grieve the Lord and hinder His cause.

It seems clear that evangelical missionary strategy will need to take more serious account of growing communist power and influence. Mission leaders just cannot afford to ignore the communist menace as they plan for the future. It is inconceivable that God would want His people to isolate themselves from the burning issues which face contemporary man.

Admittedly, numerous mission leaders are even now pondering the communist problem. They are confronted by a growing literature on the lessons learned by missionaries involved in the withdrawal from China in 1949–1953. Nor have they overlooked the record of the Protestant church in eastern Europe since World War II. This sober material is replete with grim forebodings that it is possible to undermine the future life of a national church by sheer ignorance and indifference toward twentieth-century Marxism and the intellectual ferment it generates within the society it captures.

Each of these studies has been examined in the light of Scripture and its frequent affirmation that God is the God of history. As omnipotent Providence, God is constantly at work, superintending the movements of nations and individuals, that in the end His eternal purpose might be fully realized. "All human history shall be consummated in Christ." [4]

The more one lifts up his eyes and looks on the fields of this world, white unto harvest, evaluating all in the light of Scripture, the more he begins to discern the elements of an evangelical missionary strategy suited to the world of today. What are these elements?

Knowledge is necessary

The missionary today should know the communist movement thoroughly. What is the true nature of communism? What is its basic philosophy? What are its attractions? What is its great strength? The person who has not felt the idealistic appeal and powerful incentives of the communist movement is not really qualified to speak to this generation; he is not really on its wave length. For the fact remains that many intelligent, educated people in our day honestly feel that they must

---

4. Ephesians 1:10 (J. B. Phillips' translation).

give the communist message a fair hearing. "If I were not an evangelical Christian, I'd be a Communist." Unless one can fully appreciate all that lies behind this remark of a student, he is ill prepared for missionary service abroad today.

But where is communist dogma weak? Like all man-made systems it has its glaring inadequacies. What are they?

What do Communists believe about man, his origin, nature, and destiny? Arnold Toynbee defines communism as "the worship of the collective power of man in place of the worship of God." And yet, in all of its man-worship its view of man is hopelessly inadequate. In what ways? Its most perceptive critics feel that communism is most vulnerable at this point. Are you aware of the strength and adequacy of the biblical revelation concerning man? If not, how could you help, say, a student overseas who is being drawn by communist blandishments?

One could go on. What do Communists believe about society, its structure, evolution, and future? What are Communists actually trying to do? What would your reaction be if you were told that the appeals Communists make to draw men have their counterparts in the evangelistic appeals Christ and the apostles used? What if you found that many of the methods Communists use to train their converts are found, in essence, in the Gospels? The relevancy of all this becomes abundantly clear when one realizes that communist agents and

Christian missionaries are both seeking to reach and train the same people.

What do Communists believe about Christianity, its origin, nature, and future? Lenin once said that "all modern religions and churches, and even all religious organizations are agencies of bourgeoisie reaction which serve to protect exploitation and benumb the working class." One must have a comprehensive grasp of all that lies behind these few words. Its essence is believed by millions in the world today—millions who need Christ but who are prejudiced against His witnesses. How are they to be converted if one has never taken the trouble to face and study thoroughly the seductively alluring gospel from Moscow or Peking?

The more knowledge one gains of this movement the more mental and spiritual poise he acquires. When he measures communist strength, he cries to God for a fresh revelation of His power. When he uncovers communist weaknesses, he becomes more convinced than ever that communism will never ultimately win, that it is a counterfeit of Satan, and that all who respond to its challenge will eventually be betrayed. Finally, the completely satisfying, absolute truth found within the Christian gospel and the incomparable nature and person of Jesus Christ, God's only Savior from sin, become more precious than ever. In fact, the whole experience of facing communism honestly and squarely with the Bible in hand will challenge the Christian missionary as never before to proclaim positively, authorita-

65

tively, and with winsome urgency the gospel of the Lord Jesus Christ to all men everywhere. This is the message every generation needs to hear.

Humility is essential

The more one learns of the essential nature of communism and its attraction to multitudes, the more burdened he becomes to lose his insularity and acquaint himself more fully with the world of today. This inevitably leads him to realize the enormity of the economic and social problems confronting nation after nation. For instance, to most Japanese the chief issue is not Christ or Buddha, Shinto or Science. It is land and rice. Japan, along with many other Asiatic countries, is fighting desperately for the right to exist. Recently, C. P. Fitzgerald (Professor of Far Eastern History in the Australian National University, Canberra) observed very succinctly: "In all the rice and wheat lands of Asia the governments of the newly independent states are alike threatened. Not so much by the political message of communism as by the doubt whether any other system can solve the problem of the peasant and his poverty." For this reason all eyes are fixed on China. In this connection, Mr. Fitzgerald adds: "If once the Chinese system offers an alternative more hopeful than any provided by private land tenure, it will be impossible to hold back the surge of support which local communist parties will obtain." [5]

---

5. C. P. Fitzgerald, *Flood Tide in China* (London: The Crescent Press, 1958), as quoted in *C.M.S. Newsletter*, No. 215, April, 1959.

The need everywhere is for governments to make all-out efforts to tackle their economic and social problems boldly and vigorously. In this demanding present it is a little distressing to find many evangelical Christians in North America indifferent to world needs. They like the American way of life, and since the Communists are challenging Western world leadership and their comfortable *status quo,* they tend to go along uncritically with all the anti-communist claptrap so popular today. They hardly commend themselves as responsible members of this generation.

For, say what one will, the Communists everywhere are capitalizing on the unalleviated hunger of the poverty-stricken and, for many centuries, widely exploited peoples of the earth. They are seeking with impressive devotion to share, or sometimes more accurately to impose their own peculiar brand of political and economic hope. If they succeed it will be virtually impossible to prevent a worldwide upsurge of resentment toward the Church, which has had such a privileged place in the static social structures of the past. This hostility might well be accepted as the judgment of God on a Church that failed in its day of opportunity. Past failure should lead to present contrition and humility.

Probably even less widely appreciated is the fact that the Communists are smashing hoary, idolatrous systems in the Orient. They are rooting Lamaism out of Tibet, Buddhism and ancestor worship out of China. Is this further evidence of God's activity, His judging, over-

67

throwing, and refining work in human society? If so, He is using a savage Assyrian to accomplish this. In the past, He has used Assyrians, Babylonians, Persians, and even Romans as His "servants," the chastening "rods of His anger." Later He judged them too! [6]

No one knows the role of communism in God's sovereign purpose. All the more reason why we should be slow to see the present crisis as a black-and-white issue. Perhaps God wants to use the communist movement to chasten and refine His Church. Humility truly becomes us all in the face of this possibility.

Missionary strategy implies action

Knowledge and humility are not enough. The gospel must be fully and faithfully preached to reach this generation. In detailing a comprehensive, vigorous missionary strategy, the following propositions should be embraced.

1. *Supranational.* Since the Christian movement is above national cultures, it must be divorced in the minds of the as yet totally uncommitted from all identification with the political East-West struggle of our times. In its appeal to the man in the street, the gospel must not be obscured by political or sociological overtones which awaken prejudices and close hearts. Christ's kingdom is in this world but not of it.

---

6. Isaiah 10:5, 12; Jeremiah 25:8, 9; Isaiah 44:28; Romans 13:1, etc.

2. *International.* Since the Church is worldwide, missionary teams overseas should be as international and interracial as possible. Chinese and American Christians, African and Indian brethren, must approach the uncommitted today with a genuine "we" that represents their vital union in Christ. The missionary movement must cease to be solely the possession of the white races.

3. *Sacrificial.* Since Communists are realistic as well as optimistic, they do not shrink from calling for great personal sacrifice in the light of their assured future victory. Christ does not ask for less. These are days to stress the cost of discipleship as well as the coming of the Lord. For in the end, God, not Marx, will triumph. God's future victory will amply justify all present sacrifices made in His Name, and for His sake.

4. *Communal.* Since God's purpose for this age is that His people share their common life within local congregations, the nature and function of the local church must be rediscovered and reaffirmed. Communists stress the group and the team in their program. Once and for all, the pagan selfish spirit of irresponsible individualism must be exorcised from the thinking and conduct of Christians. They belong to one another. They no longer dare live independently of one another.

5. *Societal.* Christ is interested in the whole man, his personal and family life, his community, civic and national life. Christians must refuse the tendency to

withdraw from the concerns of others. They should accept their God-given responsibility to the whole of society. The Bible speaks clearly on all these relationships. All its counsel should be meditated upon and then applied.

6. *Anticipatory*. Since Christians may witness the triumph of Marxism throughout the earth prior to the Lord's return, they should be prepared to face this eventuality. Fortunately, Scripture has not a little to say about living and witnessing in a totalitarian society. But this instruction must be dug out, mastered, and made part of the basic indoctrination given to all converts. The Church must not merely be prepared to survive in the future. It must be determined to extend and consummate God's missionary purpose.

7. *Spiritual*. Never before has the Church faced such a challenge as it does today. Never has the enemy been so determined to strip it down and make it helpless before him. Is God's answer to this challenge the promise of revival at the end of the age? Some Bible scholars think it is. But if so, few Christians appear to be interceding to that end. Without a greatly increased volume of fervent prayer support, the Church may falter in its purpose for our day and be trampled underfoot by pagan communist power.

Conclusion

Slowly but with increasing clarity, the Western world is coming to realize that there are only two major loyalties today able to lift man out of the morass of a blindly self-centered existence: loyalty to Karl Marx and loyalty to Jesus Christ. These two are irreconcilable. One is the founder of an atheistic religion, suited to the mood and material needs of modern scientific man. The other is the Son of God from heaven, the only One able to save man from either himself or his sins. There is no third loyalty.

Under whose banner do you serve?

Chapter 4: **Missions Learn from the Communist Triumph in China**

THE UNIVERSAL MISSION of the Church of Christ is caught up in the crisis of our time. In the midst of the world's current turbulence and upheaval, the Almighty is unfolding His undeviating purpose. Even before the creation of man, God anticipated a day such as this in which power and change would be worshipped as deities. He anticipated and will defeat every device of Satan, for the Lord God is sovereign. Here is the strength and comfort of His people. Yet it is possible to recognize the sovereignty of God without being fully aware of the extent of God's activity both within and without the Church.

For instance, do we recognize the enormous advances being made in the physical sciences as being part of God's plan? Or are we able to trace His sovereign operation among those nations where the testimony to His Son is seemingly so insignificant? To be specific, is

God manifestly at work in Moscow and Peking? If we believe that a sovereign God is ruling, we are obliged to accept as fact that the most seemingly chaotic events of our time have their spiritual significance.

For example, consider the communist expulsion of missionaries from China in 1950–51, and the subsequent termination of all foreign missionary activity in that vast and populous land. In the entire scope of the worldwide witness of the Church today, the China disaster was so colossal and complete that we must inevitably assume that God was seeking to speak through such a calamity to His people throughout the earth. If Christians desire to prepare themselves to serve their own generation in the will of God, they can do no better than ponder the lessons of that painful period. It is difficult not to conclude from them that Protestant missionary activity in China was under the judgment of God. David M. Paton in his severe book *Christian Missions and the Judgment of God* says that "the best of us [missionaries] left China sadly, with many happy memories, but with a sense that . . . we were wrong . . . that God found us wanting." [1] One dare not be indifferent to or seek to withdraw from the painful lessons to be learned. God has spoken; His people must pause and listen.

When it comes to evaluating the China exodus in terms of God's specific lessons to His Church, its mis-

---

1. David M. Paton, *Christian Missions and the Judgment of God* (London: S.C.M. Press, Ltd., 1953), p. 54.

sionary force and strategy, one is pressed to assume a posture and spirit of deep humility. Man's sinfulness and ignorance increase the possibility of being in error about these lessons. Rarely is our information completely adequate; seldom is our judgment both balanced and wise. There is a large measure of agreement, however, as to the lessons God was seeking to teach His people during the final decade of missionary opportunity in China. We therefore should regard these lessons with all seriousness. They have come from the Head of the Church to His people.

Lessons about Theology

Prominent in the postexilic writings of former China missionaries is their profound realization that the deepest lessons learned from God concerned faith and not service. Several reasons contributed to this conclusion. In earlier decades, when most societies were in basic doctrinal agreement, there had been a rather general movement of interdenominational societies into rural and tribal areas. Comity arrangements with denominational societies had resulted in the cities (embracing the educated and industrial classes) being turned over to the denominational societies. This was a tidy and workable arrangement as long as all societies remained true to historic biblical Christianity. Recent decades, however, saw the rise of heterodox, liberal theology, especially in America. This overflowed into China. Mission schools, colleges, and most theological seminaries came under the domination of a theology that was little more than a superficial humanism. A great deal of Western money was poured into these institutions, which attracted a host of able students. But the tragedy was that the instruction confined itself to acquainting the Chinese with the industrial and cultural achievements of the West while leaving them largely in ignorance of the Christian faith. The result was disastrous.

Bishop Stephen Neill, noted for his contribution as the Associate General Secretary of the World Council of Churches, described the situation in the following words:

> Christianity was presented [in China] much more as a program of social and political reform than as a religion of redemption. But the concepts of liberal Christianity proved in the end less dynamic than those of Marxist Communism. . . . The liberal interpretation of the Bible, from which both the prophetic and eschatological dimensions were almost wholly absent . . . produced a widespread lack of interest in theology, an almost total lack of the sense of worship, and an almost total lack of understanding of the nature of the church. [2]

Leonard M. Outerbridge, a prominent missionary of the United Church of Canada, appraised the theological failure thus:

---

2. Stephen Neill, *The Unfinished Task* (London: Lutterworth Press, 1957), p. 127.

Christianity [in China] neglected to give priority to the teaching of the first and great commandment. We sought popularity and prestige by stressing the material benefits the church had to offer. Christianity was the success religion. Too large a proportion of all Protestant missionary energies was thus expended. China willingly received every social service expression of Christianity in schools, colleges, hospitals, humanitarian aid, famine relief, and famine prevention projects. Through these agencies Christianity became popularly conceived in China as the social reform religion. But too little emphasis was placed upon the actual teaching of the message of Jesus. Our social Gospel was our only Gospel. . . .

Confronted with the rising tide of Communism, the Christian churches merely offered the Chinese a more attractive materialism than could be given by the Communists. It was in this hour that the churches were lost. The popularity of Christianity in modern China often constituted its peril. It had become soft, pleasant, and social in its application. Storm warnings should have been read in the fact that for many years the majority of the graduates of Christian schools were leaving these institutions not only without having become Christians but without any religion at all. Christian missions produced a talented but lost generation. Communism appealed to these trained young people by demanding of them greater sacrifices than Christianity, in its day of soft ease, dared demand. Students found in Communism a realism which they missed in Christianity.[3]

_____

3. Leonard M. Outerbridge, *The Lost Churches of China* (Philadelphia: The Westminster Press, 1952), pp. 159–160, 166–167.

Charles C. West, of the Ecumenical Institute, Bossey, Switzerland, writing under the pen name "Barnabas," summarized this theological failure with the damning indictment:

> Christian Liberalism turned itself easily, too easily, into Christian-Communist Liberalism in China. Christian Liberalism failed to recognize the depth of sin, and hence the need of personal salvation, humility and curbs on all social power. . . . The most vigorous Christian life in Peking today lies not in the churches but in Inter-Varsity organized student groups and sects.[4]

These admissions of theological failure need to be pondered. For in spite of Protestantism's postwar repudiation of the liberalism of the 'thirties, many church leaders in the 'sixties are still unwilling to embrace the faith "once delivered to the saints." Their preoccupation with Bultmann's demythologizing, Tillich's depersonalized theism, or Neibuhr's Christian socialism, coupled with their continued revolt against the authority and message of Scripture, indicate they have not yet discerned the hard theological lessons that came to their fellow-liberals in China.

In contrast, those missionaries who preached the biblical message of Jesus Christ and Him crucified have no such regrets. Their theology was not of man, but of God. As a result, they witnessed in China His marvel-

---

4. Barnabas, *Christian Witness in Communist China* (London: S.C.M. Press, Ltd., 1951), p. 63.

lous activity by means of this message. The lives of thousands were supernaturally transformed by His grace and His Church was planted widely throughout the length and breadth of that dark land.

And yet, even evangelical missionaries have felt the judgment of God. For many, their last impressions of Chinese brethren were of a people tragically ill-prepared to cope with the intellectual and sociological ferment generated by the communist revolution. God had not failed; but even His most faithful servants had failed to realize, and thus fulfill, the full import of the gospel. The question then arises, did they not teach the whole counsel of God contained in Scripture? It is now apparent that much of the instruction given erected a false antithesis between the spiritual and the material world. It failed abysmally to transmit to the Chinese Church the deep-rooted social concern so dynamically evidenced by the Holy Spirit through the Old Testament prophets and the New Testament apostles. It produced a form of discipleship that reflected a painfully limited viewpoint—indifference to China's social, economic, and political needs, devoid of a sense of civil responsibility. Whereas the social gospel was inadequate because of its omission of the theistic dimension, the gospel as evangelicals presented it largely ignored the biblically obvious: the gospel *has* social implications.

Today we are faced with urgent questions: Was the whole of God's purpose confined to that which took place within the walls of local churches or in evangelistic efforts among the unsaved? Did He really endorse the terrible passivity of Christians toward social problems? Was their withdrawal from the harsh realities of the suffering world outside the church walls His good, acceptable, and perfect will? Did not their negativism reinforce the Marxist thesis that the bourgeois church drugs its devotees with an all-absorbing concern for personal salvation, rendering them indifferent to the injustice and bad government of the society in which they live? Did this unreality, moving toward soporific abstractions, make for a healthy church life? Was it biblical? Did not Christ come to fill the lives of His people with vital concern and useful service on behalf of their fellow-men?

Many an evangelical missionary left China heavy with regret and burdened in heart over the incompleteness of the gospel he had preached in that needy, unhappy land. Not a few can recall instances when Chinese Christians were challenged by the Communists to work with them in righting wrongs and in remaking China. Their rapid reaction was unmistakable. Almost immediately they demonstrated their capacity to respond to the stimulus of vigorous leadership. Undoubtedly their very Christian training had given them an instinctive desire to serve others. Almost unmitigated tragedy lay in the unpalatable fact that their devotion and strength were being enlisted by a dynamically down-to-earth but ultimately utopian philosophy.

Nevertheless, to the Christian who looks for the underlying purpose of God in history there is much to be learned from the foregoing, whatever shade of theological interpretation he may favor.

Lessons about Method

1. *Living in simplicity.* Soon after his arrival in China, J. Hudson Taylor, founder of the China Inland Mission, adopted Chinese dress, lived in a Chinese-style house, and sought by every means to live close to the people to whom God had sent him. Thus the pattern was established to adopt, as far as possible, the standard of living of the local high-school teacher. "Minimize the differences between yourselves and the people to whom God sends you; eliminate all that is unnecessary." Key phrases such as these became watchwords. Many a missionary embraced them heartily and sacrificially. And yet did we live simply enough? Were we really close to the people, mentally as well as materially? Were we really friendly enough, accessible enough, and sufficiently fluent in language and culture to bridge the gulf between East and West? True, the problem isn't one of location as much as spirit, and yet many an ex-China missionary now wishes he had lived more like his Chinese or tribal colleagues in the work of the Lord. The call to Western missionaries to live in simplicity overseas has never been so loudly sounded as it is today.

2. *Recovering mobility.* The apostolic pattern of missionary service relied heavily on an essential mobility.

The Apostle Paul's peripatetic pastoral and evangelistic ministry is the classic example. Districts were opened by itinerant gospel preaching. Converts were carefully established in the faith. Congregations were organized. Then the apostles moved on into new areas. Their method was to concentrate on districts by planting churches in key cities and towns. Their follow-up programs did not necessitate prolonged residence in any one locale. They came and went, and by their absence created situations that forced converts to cling the closer to the Lord himself. They produced sturdy disciples and vigorous churches.

Unfortunately this pattern is quite contrary to even the best in human nature. It was a very real problem for missionaries in China to maintain sufficient foresight to retain mobility as a biblical *sine qua non*. So many pressures were on them constantly to settle down, and, however unintentionally, to develop the work with themselves at the center. This led quite naturally to paternalism and its attendant weaknesses. When the exodus from China took place, many an uprooted missionary thanked God for the disruption. Many prayed that if He recommissioned them, they would vow never to lose either mobility or action or loyalty to the apostolic pattern of a district-wide ministry.

3. *Conducting church finance.* There is no authority in Scripture, no precept or apostolic example, for the practice of employing converts as preachers of

81

the gospel. And this was the pattern widely followed by all missionary societies for many years in China. Since the Chinese have a propensity for fixed routines and precedents, this pattern only began to be challenged by nationals and missionaries after a series of chaotic upheavals—wars, internments, evacuations, and inflation—demonstrated beyond question its glaring weaknesses. Slowly Christian leaders became aware of the folly of such a procedure.[5] They began to recognize that converts just emerging from spiritual darkness, still surrounded by heathen influences, and imperfectly emancipated from non-Christian habits should not be recruited for service in the church on a monetary basis.

When the Communists' take over was complete, all true Christians came under severe testing. A costly price was to be paid by all who persisted in identifying themselves publicly with the cause of Jesus Christ. Nominal or weak church members melted away. Even staunch Christians felt the pressure and began to waver. It soon became evident that those paid workers who had been subsidized with foreign funds were ex-

---

5. As early as 1928, the China Inland Mission, in full consultation with the national church began to cut back its earlier commitments and adopted the policy that no new work was to be opened on this basis. Stimulus for this sweeping decision also came from the spiritual momentum generated by two notable exceptions in the C.I.M. to the subsidized program: the "people movement" led by Pastor Hsi in South Shansi (from 1880 onward) and the widespread work among the tribes of Southwest China (from 1910 onward) associated with James O. Fraser.

posed to a withering blast of communist scorn. They were singled out as "running dogs of the imperialists." Under the scorching scrutiny of public inquisition loyalty to the People's Republic was mercilessly probed. Fearfully and sometimes frantically they vehemently disowned their past associations with the foreign missionaries! Such a sudden, violent aversion, evinced by some against those who a few months earlier had been their closest associates, presented an indelibly pathetic picture. The most godly of men were not spared the infamy of shamelessly false abuse. No further evidence was necessary to sound the death knell of paternalism, at least in China!

As a result of this harsh China experience, new principles, though as old as the apostles, were adopted for the conduct of church finance. "Do not go beyond the life of the local church. If a congregation is unable to support a pastor, it would be both premature and stultifying to spiritual growth to appoint a foreign-subsidized man to care for them. Make the sole motivation for Christian service the constraint of the love of Christ. Do not deny the emerging church the privilege and blessing of looking to God himself to deepen its stewardship and supply its need." No lessons have come more clearly from China's fiery furnace than those relating to money, its use and abuse.

4. *Utilizing mass media.* This is the day of communication through mass media. The printed page, the

public address system, the motion picture film, radio and TV—all can be used effectively to proclaim Jesus Christ.

"Literature molds minds," the communist slogan bragged truthfully for once. And those of us who were in China under communist occupation would add, "Slogans too, painted on every wall; posters, hanging in every window; pictures, displayed in every shop or hall; inexpensive books, for sale in every post office; radios, blaring into every street a continuous torrent of music and words; loud speakers, filling every car on every train with the blandishments of the New Order." The pressure is ceaseless and irresistible.

Christians should utilize these means, not because the Communists employ them so effectively, but because God himself has made them available as vehicles of the message of redemption.

How rebuked we were by the profound respect the Communists paid to the human mind. They tackled the enormous task of indoctrinating the peasant classes with an astonishingly accurate conviction that untrained minds can master complicated thoughts, given teachers and time. They utilized every available means to disseminate their message.

By contrast missionary efforts were tragically slender. Limited thought-content in their tracts and books; timid attempts to use the newspapers (advangelism!) and radio: all contributed and led inexorably to a failure to reach the masses. No reflective missionary who went through the 1949–1951 "turn over" emerged unburdened by the need to capitalize on all contemporary media to convey ideas, that the despairing millions of this generation might be reached with the gospel.

Lessons about Priorities

It is the responsibility of mission leaders to define strategic priorities that the strength and skills of their missionary force might be put to the best possible use. It is always easy to waste time and dissipate strength in peripheral matters. Nowhere is it easier to play at busyness (much ado about nothing) than on the mission field. Priorities must be prayerfully fixed and workers must be carefully allotted to strategic tasks most consonant with their gifts and training. The China experience caused many a mission leader to have "second thoughts" after the door to further missionary service in that land was irrevocably closed.

What is top priority? "The unreached: the gospel must be preached to every creature." Yes, but which segment of the unreached is the responsibility of the foreign missionary force? What is the over-all strategic concept of a missionary society? "The planting of a national church that will accept and discharge the responsibility for evangelizing the rest of its countrymen." Yes, but where should this church be established in strength? "In the cities, among the educated classes, the two per cent that will produce the future leaders of the nation." But does this not overlook rural and tribal peoples? "By no means. Follow the sovereign leading of the Spirit and you will discover that He does not follow a rigid, undeviating pattern. He may guide unmistakably that a certain rural area or despised tribe become the object of His electing grace." Then all talk of strategy and priorities is irrelevant? "No. The Apostle Paul worked the cosmopolitan cities, the university and commercial centers, but did not resist the unusual leading of the Lord that occasionally took him to rural areas."

Some might argue that theoretical discussions of mission strategy are pointless. The allegation is that in actual practice personal and circumstantial factors often largely dictate policy. There is no little truth to this melancholy charge. Non-strategic factors often tend to blur and distort strategic planning. Unless field leadership is able to keep ultimate goals rigidly in view, planning tends to degenerate, permitting every man to do what appears right in his own eyes.

This undoubtedly occurred in China. Great cities had weak churches. The student classes, so productive in communist leadership, were largely neglected until it was a case of "too little, too late." Whereas the more aggressive and able Chinese were drawn from their villages to urban centers, mission societies sent many of their best men to work in rural areas. Tribal and Tibetan work tended to be glamorized out of all proportion to the numbers of souls actually involved. All in all, strategic considerations seemed to play little

86

part in the over-all development of the work. As a result, when the evacuation took place, it was sadly realized that insufficient emphasis had been placed on training a vigorous and able leadership for the national churches. The few small evangelical training schools that existed were of poor academic quality. With a few notable exceptions, such as the Kiangwan Bible Seminary, missionary vision had not been widely imparted.

Why were there so few churches and men willing to evangelize areas within China and beyond its borders in the Far East? At the time of the evacuation in 1951, missionary work in the Orient was almost solely a Western activity. The Apostle Paul planted some churches that became notably missionary-minded. Many an ex-China missionary now wishes that decades earlier Protestant missions had been more priority-minded, more desirous of producing a responsible leadership that would have taken the lead in church extension in the Far East. With the coming of the Communists this opportunity to produce key men and impart missionary vision has been ended—by the Lord of the harvest. May God forgive the Western missionary, who by his limited vision provided the Communists with some of their most effective propaganda thrusts: "Only white men are missionaries. Christianity is the religion of the white imperialists. When imperialism is destroyed, Christianity will wither and die. The Asian who becomes a Christian turns his back on his home, his people, and his country."

Conclusion—The Spiritual Lesson

The most serious communist charge leveled against missionaries was that they were the agents of imperialism. This was an oblique attack intended to discredit and undercut all the positive social and spiritual good the missionary movement had brought to China. But when this propaganda assault was supported by selective and subtle appeals to some of the more sordid events in the previous hundred years of Western machinations in the Orient—the Opium Wars, the "incidents" that led to various uprisings, and other international disturbances—missionaries became uneasy. Some tended to lose sight of the fact that they had come to China at the call of God. Not a few bowed to the force of these distorted charges. They began to fear they had been the unconscious pawns of a studied Western cultural and political penetration of China. Although previously largely disinterested in politics, they now came to fear they had been political symbols, who by their very presence had influenced the Chinese against China's best interests. The more they pondered these implications the more distressed they became. "The day of the foreign missionary is over—perhaps throughout the Far East"—this now became their mournful dirge.

In contrast, other missionaries reacted against this communist propaganda assault with much indignation and wild generalizations. "Our motives have been pure. God's blessing has been on our work. What we have said and done has been at His bidding. What wrong have we done?" They unfortunately erred on the side of losing a sense of historic perspective. Thinking that to confess failure would reflect on Christ, they lost the grace of self-criticism. Their self-justifying refutations appeared almost to confirm communist propaganda. They revealed their inability to appreciate the revolutionary situation that had engulfed China including themselves. Their pride was pricked. This was apparent to the Chinese. As a result their righteous indignation only served to isolate them from the Chinese church. All in all, the Communists executed a diabolically clever stroke when they pinned the imperialist label on Western missionaries.

All this points up the final lesson, the spiritual lesson we must learn from the mass exodus of missionaries from China. This great crisis demonstrated that the Western missionary today is a marked man. He is handicapped by history. He represents a segment of the world which is nervously on the defensive. He is the symbol of racial and color conflict. He is the target of jealous nationalist resentment. He must forever face the strain of discrimination and the possibility of expulsion. He must be prepared to bear the reproach of Christ in a singular fashion common to none else.

But he can continue to rejoice! Regardless of how despised he may be by this generation, he nevertheless believes in God's sovereignty. God is in control of history, including the harrowing present. God has ordained that His witnesses evangelize this generation, despite its materialism and revolutionary climate. The very pilgrim nature of His witnesses is one of the wonderful assets He has bestowed on the missionary movement today. True, His witnesses have no standing, no prestige, no power-of-themselves. But they are symbols of the universality of the gospel. They represent the Lord Jesus Christ whose kingdom is "not of this world." Therefore they can rejoice in their high calling, while putting their entire heart and will into the task of proclaiming Christ to men.

Chapter 5: **The Church Witnesses in Communist China**

IT IS NOW MORE THAN TEN YEARS since foreign missionary societies were obliged to withdraw from China. When they bid their Chinese brethren a final *"Tsai-huei p'ing-an,"* their words "May-we-meet-again-in-peace!" doubtless had reference more to the final reunion in the Lord's presence in glory than to any anticipated future reunion on this earth. Many felt that China's modern missionary era, which began with Robert Morrison in 1807, had come to an end.

Since 1951, revolutionary changes have drastically altered the worldwide missionary outreach of the Church. The recent role of societies that formerly served in China is a thrilling record of redeployment by a sovereign God. Nooks and crannies in the countries of the Far East that had been bypassed in the general missionary advance of earlier decades have now been penetrated with the gospel by ex-China missionaries and their societies. These mopping-up operations may possibly be the final phase of the activities of Western missionaries in the Orient prior to the return of Christ. Redeployment indeed! God is at work today that He might consummate His missionary purpose tomorrow.

But what of the Church left behind in China? How has she fared? What has been her experience in the intervening years? What has she learned as a result of her awful ordeal? Questions such as these come to the fore whenever ex-China missionaries meet together and discuss the "old days." Fortunately, they do not have to speculate as to what is actually taking place in China. Bits of information have been filtering through the bamboo curtain from all parts of China. These have been collated and studied, and reports have been issued. In fact, a book has been written on the subject by Leslie T. Lyall, the Candidate Secretary for Great Britain of the China Inland Mission. This book describes the tragic experiences of the Church in China under communist rule since 1950.[1]

What has been the pattern of the life of this Church? Many would agree that it has been the object of "a carefully planned and cleverly executed" government program to eliminate it as a spiritual force without completely destroying its physical existence. Since in a com-

---

1. *Come Wind, Come Weather* (Chicago: Moody Press, 1960). Unfortunately, this book is insufficiently critical of the many-sided failure of missionaries in preparing nationals to face the problem of living and surviving in a communist society.

munist state all must actively support the "socialist reconstruction" of society, the organized church has been cajoled by flattery, deceived by lies, swayed by fear, and bent to the will of the state. "The church must lean to one side," Chairman Mao bluntly decreed, and great pressures have been used to bring this about.

Nevertheless, a sturdy evangelical remnant has survived this first decade of persistent pressure and persecution. It offers a message for us all. Although earlier regarded as "that obstinate element" by its liberal Protestant detractors, it is becoming increasingly apparent that vital Christianity in China today has its strongest roots in the evangelical segment within the Protestant Church. We do well to ponder its message to the Church "outside." The chief elements of this message follow.

Intellectual Preparation

We discovered gaps in our knowledge. It is well-nigh impossible to comprehend the depth and extent of the intellectual ferment generated by a communist-style revolution. Once the Communists seize political power they launch a vast program of indoctrination. Everyone is obliged to take part, Christians included. Street meetings, lectures in the public squares, neighborhood study classes, private reading assignments, discussion groups in industries—all supplement the formal educational system of the state. Day after day, week after week, month after month, a torrent of new ideas is poured into the minds of the people. Since the heart of the Communist system is avowedly atheistic, this indoctrination provokes great tension within the minds of Christians. Those who have survived and remained loyal to Christ would attribute the victory to His grace alone. But they would also thank Him that he used the following factors to strengthen them in their trial.

1. *Personal surrender: the lordship of Christ is primary.* Only those Chinese Christians who are fully surrendered to Christ have been serene in their hearts. They see things in true perspective. They remain unmoved by what evil men say or do. They see but one divine Cause which admits no bitterness toward the oppressive atheists, nor any entanglement with second causes. God is working all things together for good to those who love Him. But those Christians whose hearts were divided, whose love had not yet ripened into that mature faith which counts on constant fellowship with Him in whom we are complete, became restless and unable to see the Lord clearly when they needed Him most. Like Peter of Galilee, they were wholly taken up with the storm-tossed waves which threatened to engulf them. Uncertain of the future, unmindful of the past, they began to drown in unbelief.

2. *Biblical orientation: Christianity and Marxism are irreconcilable.* Christians with an integrated knowledge of the Word of God were uniquely conditioned to maintain intellectual poise and recognize the inadequacies of communist dogma. They alone were

equipped to see through its defective view of man, its careless dismissal of the problem of evil, its unrealistic faith in human perfectibility, and its lack of an adequate personal or social ethic. All in all, scientific materialism, no matter how plausibly presented, cannot satisfactorily answer man's basic questions about the world (How and where did it originate?), human life (Who am I and what am I here for?), and the future (What happens to me after death?). Christians poorly instructed in the fundamentals of the faith were soon swept away by the deluge of relentless and well-taught communist propaganda.

3. *Corporate life: the vital contribution of the local church.* Those Christians in China who have maintained contact with their fellow-Christians have discovered how essential this has been to their personal survival. Being soundly taught in the nature and function of the local church, they were determined to participate with fellow-Christians in a worshipful sharing of the Lord in their midst. By petition and intercession, by exhortation and counsel, they strengthened one another. Thus, by sharing, they came to understand in a new way the true meaning of the New Testament term *koinonia*—fellowship in the gospel. In contrast, those who in ignorance or fear failed to meet together were far more vulnerable to communist blandishments. "Two are better than one; . . . For if they fall, one will lift up his fellow; but woe to him who is alone when he falls . . ." (Ecclesiastes 4:9, 10).

95

4. *Specific indoctrination: the peril of compromise.*
The controversy arising around Pastor Wang Ming-
tao of Peking, which has lasted from 1953 until now,
has torn the Chinese Church apart. This resolute
evangelical Christian leader precipitated a major crisis
by his determination to remain fully loyal to his Lord
despite the cost involved. During World War II he
gained nation-wide prominence by his courageous opposition to the Japanese. When later the Communists
endeavored to force all Protestant churches into a single
amalgamation, without any genuinely scriptural basis or
authority, he was resolutely opposed to such a betrayal.
Thus he soon became Public Enemy Number One
in the eyes of those men, inside the church and outside of it, who were trying to make the church the docile
agent of the state. Fortunately, Pastor Wang received
worldwide attention as he called for the uncompromis-
ing obedience of all evangelicals in the midst of a com-
promising Church. His cry was that the Church dare
not come to terms with an atheistic state. Efforts were
made to break him by slander in the scurrilous religious press, by imprisonment and brain-washing tech-
niques, by forcing him to sign false confessions, and by
attacking his family. At times it seemed as though
Pastor Wang was wavering. To this day, however, he
continues faithful to the Lord. His courage has strengthened many.

But what can we learn from his ordeal? Simply that
the evangelical church in a totalitarian state must be

prepared to stand against all attacks, including those backed by a sub-biblical theology and coming from within the professing church. Even more bluntly, the evangelical must be prepared to resist an inclusivist ecumenical church which subordinates biblical authority to the temporary expediency of apparent survival. The State is determined that all Christians be united in an organization it can control. All its propaganda pressure is aimed to achieve this end. The Church must prepare itself beforehand. It must know what the Bible says concerning co-operation with an unbelieving system or society, together with the more subtle perils of theological compromise.

Spiritual Vulnerability

We tolerated areas of weakness in our hearts. Reviewing the crisis that came to the Church over the vigorous testimony of Wang Ming-tao, one is appalled at the theologically conservative leaders who joined with the liberals in crying for his blood. Why did this happen? What made his former associates in the ministry turn on him? What means did the Communists use to enlist their support? What vulnerable areas did they uncover in the lives of men who had earlier been so strong for Christ and His Word? The accumulated evidence points to four main areas.

1. *Pull of family.* Many Christians were willing to pay any price to remain true to their Lord. Some, however, found the price too high when their own family

was involved. They began to tolerate compromise when it cropped up in the lives of their loved ones. The fear that one's stand might cause his beloved wife or children to suffer broke some. Others collapsed through harboring worldly ambitions for their children. One prominent evangelical is a case in point. Some observers feel that this man's son, who was interested in communism, made his indulgent father ambitious for him to advance in the new state. God alone knows a man's full motive, but the fact remains that he became a willing helper in the state program to suppress evangelical opposition to the state church.

2. *Pull of nationalism.* Nationalism has been described as "the one sin Christians never confess." Few Christians appear to get to the place the Apostle Paul attained where they are willing to die to their national and cultural origins that they might win others to Christ (see I Cor. 9:20–22). We can all manifest great blindness when it comes to distinguishing between the claims of Caesar and the claims of Christ. The Communists have discovered this. In the U.S.S.R. they failed to destroy the Church through either physical force or persuasive propaganda. But when the war situation grew desperate in 1941, and when Stalin desperately needed a means whereby he could rally the spirit of the masses (who were not interested in fighting for the survival of communism), he appealed to the Orthodox Church to call the people to a "holy war to protect Mother Russia." Sergei, the

Patriarch, eagerly responded. Overnight the war was transformed into a crusade. Stalin had stumbled on an area of vulnerability. Official policy of the Russian church states: "The orthodox clergy and laity are utterly loyal to the Soviet power. We are Russians. Our religion is Russia's national religion. Whoever touches Russia, touches the Russian Church and its faithful." [2] Even today the church in the U.S.S.R. is not unwilling to further Soviet aggression. Her uncrucified nationalism has made this possible.

In China the same oblique approach was used with devastating results. Chinese Christians naturally love their country. When the Communists stirred up the latent, elemental group loyalty of Chinese nationalism, there was a strong response. Here was an area the Cross had not yet marked. Even as early as 1952 the state church could boast: "The loyalty of Christians and their zeal for their nation has been raised very high. They recognize that love for one's country and love for the church are one and the same thing. Therefore all Christians fervently enter into all the efforts of the Oppose-America-Aid-Korea Movement." [3] Not Christ, but Caesar has triumphed!

3. *Pull of conscience.* The evangelical movement in China largely reflected that segment of Protestantism in the homelands from which its missionaries had

---

2. Pierre van Paassen, *Visions Rise and Change* (New York: The Dial Press, 1955), pp. 153, 311, 314.

3. Lyall, *op. cit.*, p. 22.

come. Its strengths and its weaknesses were largely non-Chinese in origin. Among these was an incomplete and inadequate understanding of the place and purpose of the Church in society. Kiang Wen-han, a Chinese church leader, exposed this weakness when he stated: "The fundamentalists escape existential problems by separating so-called spiritual life from everyday practical life, with the result that in the tide of revolution they very easily become the tool of reactionary forces." [4] While not every Chinese Christian would agree with him, many felt that as Christians they had been trained to ignore social problems while concentrating on evangelism. When the Communists came with their plans for putting every citizen to work in organizing society, they tended to be almost too responsive in reaction against their earlier lack of concern. Of course, this resulted in their committing themselves far beyond what was actually required of them. They thus got beyond their depth too quickly. Their hearts went ahead of their heads. They lost their sense of scriptural perspective. This led to compromise and a weakening of their primary obligation to witness to Jesus Christ.

4. *Pull of pride.* People the world over desire to be accepted and recognized as first-class citizens. Unfortunately, Christians are no exception to this rule. Under the regime of Chiang Kai-shek, Protestantism

---

4. *Christianity and Marx-Leninism,* trans. Frank L. Cooley (New York: Missionary Research Library, 1952), p. 4.

had position, power, and influence in Chinese society. The Christian movement was respected; by 1949 it had become almost the popular thing to attend church. Church leaders became accustomed to the approval of their fellow-men. Then the Communists came. The church was fearful of persecution. The best hope was that it might be regarded as a neutral force in the new society. Imagine the surprise then that came to the church when its leaders were respectfully treated and frequently consulted by the communist leaders. Christians were still regarded as first-class citizens! What relief this brought. All that the Bible says about heavenly citizenship, about the irreconcilable differences in ultimate goals that should exist between the Christian and the world, about the perils of the "pride of life"—all was brushed aside in the desire to maintain the apparent approval of the Communists. As a result, the Church lost its freedom to be the mouthpiece of God in the new society. It became uncritical and tolerant of atheistic power. The deceitfulness of pride proved the undoing of the people of God.

5. *Pull of Satan*. Nothing has caused friends of the Church in China more dismay and concern than the frightening way in which it succumbed, in such large measure, to the pressure of the state to conduct "accusation meetings" among its own membership. In no aspect of their total program for bending the Church to their will have the Communists shown more diabolical skill. Making parody of the exhortation of James

5:16 to confess one's faults to one another, they succeeded in getting Christians to destroy one another by lies, slander, character assassination, and unimaginable abuse. Many noble souls refused to go along with this. In consequence they suffered because of their love for fellow Christians. Some committed suicide rather than participate in cleverly contrived public spectacles of Christians deliberately betraying one another. There were others who failed their Christian friends and their Lord in the meetings. How this could have happened in a Chinese society which for hundreds of years gloried in family loyalty, and in a living Church indwelt by the Holy Spirit, is a mystery that only eternity will reveal. Suffice it to say, there must have been something defective in their understanding of the true nature of the Church as revealed in Scripture. Clearly, such failures were scarcely a convincing demonstration of the power of God to the non-Christian. Such a flagrant denial of the oneness of the Body of Christ can only be erased by the grace of God and the confession of His people. But, had the Church been better trained would it have capitulated so completely? Many an ex-China missionary has asked himself this question in the depths of his own heart.

Evangelistic Outreach

We were inadequately trained for a full-orbed witness. Fortunately, the picture of the Church in China is not one of unrelieved darkness. Many of God's people have remained true to Christ. Although many have been imprisoned and broken, and others have gained a martyr's crown, there is still a witnessing Church in China today. Christ is being preached, people are becoming Christians, and God's purpose for worldwide witness is being extended. But the Church now wishes that it had been better prepared to meet the heavy demands made on it. Reviewing its pre-communist past, it sadly realizes that it was insufficiently prepared in the following crucial areas.

1. *Personal evangelism.* Although recent government decrees forbid "cottage meetings," gatherings in homes to "break bread," and all religious activities "outside the jurisdiction of the Three-Self Movement" (The State Church), there has been no proscription against doing personal work. No communist state in the world has attempted to make personal witnessing illegal. In fact, this is the chief means being used in communist countries today to proclaim Jesus Christ. A report (1954) from remote Inner Mongolia states, "It has been found very difficult to do anything but personal work, but there have been some conversions among the nomads." Sadly, the Church has been compelled to recognize its lack of training for this type of outreach! Today the strategic importance of personal evengelism is becoming increasingly central in the thinking of mission strategists the world over. The experience of the Chinese church has served to demonstrate this. Although all Christians do not have the same God-given

103

ministry, all are indwelt by the Holy Spirit and are thus capable of being used to win others.

2. *Leadership training.* During the years preceding the communist take over, there were some excellent Christian training schools functioning in China. Despite the upheavals of war, they trained many for leadership in the church. Some of these graduates formed indigenous missionary societies to take the gospel to remote areas in West China and Central Asia. Others began to produce Christian literature. Looking back now, however, it is apparent that these efforts were most inadequate. In the field of training men for the pastorate, for missions, and for literature work, the Western missionary movement was often lacking in vision. Its policy of paternalism hindered the rapid development of a vigorous church. Whereas the Chinese themselves were aware of the growing communist menace, Westerners tended to dismiss it. They did not train church leaders to cope with the challenge issued by persuasive communist propaganda. They did not challenge any to produce a literature that would deal with the problem. They trained men as they themselves had been trained, with limited Christian perspective on the local church's place in society. To illustrate: great tribal churches were led by men who were abysmally indifferent to the corruption around them—opium traffic, feudal slavery, rapacious landlords, social injustice—and this in areas where the Church repre-

sented a significant and sizeable segment in the total society. In the end, God judged His people and drove out the foreigners who had reproduced in the minds of their converts their own incomplete understanding of the Church and its message to society. Today, Christians in China must perforce participate in the reconstruction of society. These are hard lessons, but they need to be weighed carefully.

3. *Priesthood of believers.* It is a Protestant and biblical concept that all Christians are priests. All have direct access to God the Father through the Son. All have been given spiritual gifts, to be exercised for the edification of the Body of Christ and the advancement of the kingdom of God. It is recognized of course, that some may be able to give their full time directly to the Lord's service, while others may only be able to serve part-time. The Church, however, dare not allow the false dichotomy of clergy vs. laity to get out-of-hand. In a communist society, if the clergy have too much power or too much responsibility, they become terribly exposed to communist pressure. And the pressure can both break them and destroy the Church *in toto*. Also, lay Christians can all too easily surrender their priesthood and become nonproductive, noncontributing members of their local churches. This is what took place in China. In retrospect, many Chinese Christians wish they had been more aware of personal responsibility to the local church, to strengthen its life

105

and witness—every Christian a worker, every Christian a priest, every Christian a functioning member of the Body of Christ.

Trusting in Divine Grace

One dare not forget God and His resources in times such as these. Those who have been enabled to serve Him acceptably in the crisis in China today are those who have most counted on His grace and willingness to answer prayer. They have discovered that Communists are sinners, too, in need of a Christian witness. They have discovered that Communists are never fully consistent in the application of their own policies. They have discovered that words spoken in love can reach the most bigoted and needy and cause God's purpose to go forward, despite all that Antichrist may do to hinder. But only the venturesome, the men of faith, will rise to make this the Church's finest hour. *The greatest lesson the Church in China has to share with us is this: it is possible to do the will of God and serve Him acceptably in a communist society.*

True, it may not be possible to serve God in the pattern to which we are accustomed here in the West, with freedom of assembly, freedom of speech, and other freedoms so precious to us. But all of God's commands for holy and righteous living and for evangelistic outreach are always practicable and workable, no matter what the pressures may be. God knew all about com-

106

munism when He inspired the writing of the Holy Scriptures. He has not been caught off guard. And His word to His people in these dark days ever remains: "Occupy till I come." In our obedience we discover His faithfulness.

Part II. The Church in Tension

Chapter 6: Ecumenical Christianity and Missions

THE NINETEENTH CENTURY has been described by Church historian K. S. Latourette as "The Great Century" of Protestant missions. At its beginning there were almost no missionary societies. At its close Protestant churches were recruiting their young people for overseas service under the slogan, "The Evangelization of the World in This Generation." Almost sixty generations of Christians had come and gone since Christ had issued the Great Commission, but they then felt that their generation could and should "evangelize to a finish" and "bring back the King." By 1900 Protestant Christianity was worldwide. Many felt that the time had come to take steps to convene a conference which would be so complete in its representation of every stream in Protestantism that comprehensive plans might be made "for the immediate occupation of all unoccupied fields."

111

This conference, eventually convened at Edinburgh in 1910, set the stage for an entirely new and unforeseen epoch—that of the Ecumenical Movement. There are many Protestant leaders today who feel that if present trends continue, the twentieth century will prove even more notable than the nineteenth century. These leaders foresee the Ecumenical Movement fully realizing its highest aspirations and achieving its most elusive goals.

What is this movement? How did it begin? What is its major activity? What are its goals? Does its emergence at this time have any eschatological significance? There seems little doubt that its worldwide character affects, and in part determines, current missionary strategy.

But what attitude should the evangelical student personally assume as he surveys its onward march? Since it professes to represent the vanguard of Christianity in this generation, it should first be understood.

Some Definitions

In the midst of World War II, in April 1942, William Temple was consecrated Archbishop of Canterbury. At that time, while contemplating the world's political and cultural disintegration, he could find only a single reconciling, uniting force: the Church of Jesus Christ. What he then said captured the imagination of many and has been widely quoted ever since. To him, the worldwide church, existing in fragmentation in many lands, consisting of many races and speaking many tongues, was "the great new fact of our era."

It might seem strange to refer to this as a great discovery, for the essential oneness of the Church is an ancient, biblical concept. But to Archbishop Temple, the existence of the worldwide visible Church was more than merely the cradle of a spiritual entity. He was struck by its tremendous potential, despite the diverse streams that make up its fullness. Its worldwide fellowship was to him, in short, an "Ecumenical Movement."

But why use the term "ecumenical" and why describe the church as a "movement"? The word ecumenical is an Anglicized adjective of the ancient Greek noun *oikoumene*, meaning "the inhabited earth." It appears frequently (15 times) in the Greek New Testament and was used (in the fourth century of the Christian era) to designate those great Church Councils which represented the entire church, and debated doctrinal and other church concerns for the acceptance of all. The word describes the universality and catholicity of God's people scattered throughout the earth. It is an improvement on the word "international," since it avoids reference to man-made, national differences.

The word "movement" should be understood, too. Some of its leaders are careful to affirm that it is "not primarily a matter of complex organization. It is much more an attitude, a conviction, a way of understanding

113

the Church's task, and a new Christian reformation." [1] What does this mean? A movement involves direction, growth, adaptation, and change. All these are fundamental to the Ecumenical Movement.

Expressed Goals of the Ecumenical Movement

The very lofty ideals expressed in the official literature of this movement are impressive. Three dominant convictions appear again and again. First, God desires to use the worldwide Church to "extend the gospel of reconciliation to all generations and nations." Second, this task is "drastically and inexcusably hindered by the divisions of classes, races, and denominations within the church." Third, the unity of the church "can be made more manifest" and "its task more effective" by a "renewal of the corporate faith, worship, and discipline of the Christian church at large, and the local congregation in particular."

It is a movement in that its Christianity is not denominational or sectarian, national or parochial. "Its hallmark is its wholeness and extensiveness, as contrasted with the brokenness and limited range of much familiar Christianity." Christians in the Ecumenical

1. J. Robert Nelson (Dean of Vanderbilt's Divinity School), "Ecumenical Christianity," *The Christian Mission Today*, ed. The Joint Section of Education and Cultivation of the Board of Missions of the Methodist Church (Nashville: Abingdon Press, 1960), p. 223. Quotations in the next few paragraphs are taken from this chapter. It is felt that the thoughts, even words, of one of its outstanding leaders should be given to present the Ecumenical Movement in the best possible light.

Movement are not primarily desirous of encouraging cooperation between existing churches. Cooperation is of secondary importance to them. They rather desire to "grasp the fulness of the Gospel and of Christian doctrine." By this is meant an eagerness to enter into the life and worship, the doctrine and practice of all Christian bodies, young and old, scattered throughout the whole earth. They are "impatient with every barrier which prevents Christians as individuals or groups from enjoying unrestricted fellowship with all others."

They argue that the Church is one, that it is evolving, growing, developing. Their great debate centers over the variety of answers they themselves give to the fundamental question: "What is the nature of the unity we seek?" They are deeply concerned that Christ prayed for the unity of His people "that the world may believe . . . that the world may know . . . that thou hast sent me" (John 17:21, 23). But how to make this oneness evident and visible to the world is the great problem. They believe God is with them even though they do not know the ultimate destination of the movement. "This is one mark of the glory of the Ecumenical Movement. In it, in accord with the measure of our faith and of our obedience to the Holy Spirit, we are being led by God into that kind of life that He wills for His Church." [2]

The literature of the Ecumenical Movement is exten-

---

2. W. Richey Hogg, *One World One Mission* (New York: Friendship Press, 1960), p. 89.

sive. Its atmosphere is one of friendly, though serious debate. A tremendous intellectual ferment has been generated by burdened minds, united in a crusade whose direction is approved, but whose ultimate goals are only dimly perceived.

They ask one another hard and basic questions. What makes a man a member of the Church anyway? How can we have a theological basis of faith when we are seeking to cross all theological lines to enter into the total experience of all the churches in Christendom? How can we achieve the unity we desire, but cannot yet describe? Would a "council for cooperation" be sufficient above the denominational level? "To some of us manifest unity means visible, corporate, local unity" writes Visser 't Hooft. To others there can and should be legitimate diversities in one united world Church. But which loyalty should have precedence: ecumenical, denominational, or local? What attitude should we have toward fundamentalist sects, Roman Catholics, Southern Baptists, and Missouri Synod Lutherans?

The Ecumenical Movement, however, is more than a debating society. They are tackling seriously such divisive and controversial issues as racial segregation in churches, class stratification in church life, and denominational divisions. In recent decades, hardly a year passes without the consummation of a church union somewhere. A perusal of an annual report of their interdenominational "Church World Service" will impress one with their serious and costly efforts—feeding the hungry, healing the sick, and helping in various other ways by seeking "to be a Christian presence" throughout the world. They feel that the longer they delay the quest for unity the longer they will remain weak. One almost irresistible argument they frequently use is that "no fragment of the universal church, no denomination or communion by itself, can embody and express the richness and fulness of the Gospel, of worship and devotion, of theology and ethics." To perpetuate divisions is to tolerate the undernourishment of the whole church and the frustration of its unexpressed "love for the brethren." Then, too, the more divided the church the weaker its witness to the world on matters touching social justice and human dignity. As divided churches "our witness is heard by the world, not as a united, compelling voice, but as a confused and discordant babble." Finally, they argue, "We cannot proclaim a reconciling Christ to the world if we Christians are not fully reconciled among ourselves."

There are outstanding men in this movement. They have sought to sense the need of the church as they know it throughout the world, and do something about it. They want to be constructive and helpful. As one of them has said, "Every attitude, assertion, or activity which we call ecumenical must be subjected to judgment by the criterion of Jesus Christ our Lord." One cannot dismiss this movement with a syllogism or two, or a categorical judgment, much less a contemptuous sneer, as some evangelical Christians mistakenly have done. And yet the whole movement poses the gravest of problems. In order to appreciate them fully, it is necessary to review the record of its historical development. It will be discovered that the movement hinges very largely around the worldwide missionary outreach of the church.

History

The Edinburgh Conference of 1910 was the first representatively worldwide interdenominational missionary conference. Under the leadership of Dr. John R. Mott, the slogan, "The Evangelization of the World in This Generation" had basic biblical connotations. Most of those attending believed that all men were lost, and that Christ died for all; the gospel, therefore, must be preached to all. "Most participants seemed to take for granted that the Great Commission of Christ (Matthew 28:19) was the only basis needed for the missionary enterprise . . . the missionary obligation was considered a self-evident axiom to be obeyed, not to be questioned." [3] This was essentially a "strategy conference," whose purpose was to ensure that the missionary task might be accomplished as efficiently and quickly as possible. In order to maintain a sense of continuity for all participating societies, a Continuation Committee was formed. It began to function effectively after its May, 1911 meeting at Auckland Castle, under

3. Gerald H. Anderson, ed., *The Theology of the Christian Mission* (New York: McGraw-Hill Book Company, 1961), p. 5.

the sympathetic eye of the Bishop of Durham, Dr. H. C. G. Moule, one of the great evangelical leaders of his day. After spasmodic growth it brought into being the International Missionary Council in 1921, at Lake Mohawk, New York.

But the years immediately following were filled with catastrophic upheaval and vast changes. World War I and its tragic aftermath, the growth of secularism hand in hand with liberal theology, the emergence of the Social Gospel movement,[4] and the great increase and popularity of destructive biblical criticism—each contributed to a tremendous shift in emphasis among a very articulate and able segment of the church's younger leadership. The next great world conference was held in Jerusalem in 1928, at the height of a worldwide economic boom that burst a few months later, ushering in "the great depression."

Jerusalem differed greatly from Edinburgh. No longer was there a clear-cut biblical simplicity. Evangelical delegates discovered a growing desire on the part of the liberals to approach the non-Christian religions with a sympathy and appreciation foreign to New Testament standards. When mission goals were discussed, it was revealed that many felt the missionary movement should be more "this worldly" in its objectives. Living without Christ now seemed more tragic

---

4. In the year 1912 Walter Rauschenbusch published his famous book, *Christianizing the Social Order*. This volume greatly influenced the preaching of the American Protestant pulpit away from the message of the grace of God in Christ.

than dying without Christ. "Our message is Jesus Christ; we dare not give less, and we cannot give more"—these words of William Temple helped to unite conservatives and liberals at this conference, but as Bishop Neill sagely remarked, "Evangelism was no longer in the center of the picture, and no more was heard of 'the evangelization of the world in this generation.' " [5]

Bishop Stephen Neill, prominent in the activities of the World Council of Churches, has stated that a case could be made out for regarding the deliberations of the Jerusalem Conference as "the nadir of the modern missionary movement." His explanation: "This was the moment at which liberal theology exercised its most fatal influence on missionary thinking, the lowest valley out of which the missionary movement has ever since been trying to make its way." [6]

In the years immediately following Jerusalem, this new shift in emphasis gained many adherents and became an over-all trend—chiefly through what came to be known as the Laymen's Missionary Inquiry. Dr. W. B. Hocking, a Harvard philosophy professor, led a group of prominent laymen on a tour of world mission fields at the conclusion of which he wrote a book entitled, *Rethinking Missions*.[7] Years later Dr. Hocking wrote in retrospect:

---

5. Stephen Neill, *The Unfinished Task* (London: Lutterworth Press, 1957), p. 152.

6. *Ibid.*, p. 151.

7. New York: Harper and Brothers, 1932.

Our commission for the Laymen's Inquiry, which studied missions around the world two and a half decades ago, fortunately included two types of mind, and both on the alert. We had our conservatives holding to the "Only Way" principle as a matter not alone of loyalty but of plain common sense— you either accept the saving work of Christ, done once for all, or you don't; Christ cannot be generalized nor watered down by theological appeasement. These members were reasonably worried by the broad net which others, including the chairman, tended to cast—by their respectful care for and interest in local pieties, as if for them the word "superstition" had ceased to have a distinctive meaning. They were troubled when any of us went so far as to take part in a service of worship of Hindu or Parsee origin; and especially so when one of our women members, who shall remain forever unidentified, accepted an invitation on the spot to join a group of Hindu women dancing at a festival of Rama to celebrate the full moon! [8]

The recommendations of this inquiry were published under the title *Rethinking Missions*. Among other recommendations they included: (1) Give prominence to the social gospel—"the primary business of the missionary in the future is to permeate the personal life of the individual and the fabric of human society with creative ideals and energies . . . rather than to build a church as an institution to stand out as an entity in

8. *The Christian Century*, March 29, 1955, p. 268. Copyright 1955 Christian Century Foundation. Reprinted by permission.

itself apart from the larger whole of society" (pp. 108, 109). (2) Remove evangelism from schools and medical work—"the time has come to set the educational and other philanthropic aspects of mission work free from organized responsibility to the work of conscious and direct evangelism" (p. 70). (3) Regard non-Christian religions and their devotees as fellow-seekers after truth—"the missionary will look forward, not to the destruction of these religions, but to their continued co-existence with Christianity, each stimulating the other in growth toward the ultimate goal, unity in the completest religious truth" (pp. 443, 444). (4) Recruit, train, and appoint only liberal-minded missionaries—"a much more critical selection of candidates should be made . . . to prepare for the transition from the temporary work of church planting, pioneer work in medicine, education and the training of leaders—to the permanent function of promoting world understanding and unity on a spiritual level through the ambassadorship of these relatively few highly equipped persons . . ." (p. 328); and (5) unify all mission boards under one general administration—"the most urgent need is the adoption and rigid enforcement, in all fields, of a definite policy of concentration of personnel and resources" (p. 304).

Many were enthusiastic about this report. To them it was evident that "Modernists are not now a minority in Protestant leadership" (*Christian Century*). But many evangelicals reacted with dismay. The report's publication was a signal to liberal forces within denominations and missionary societies to reach for the control of their organizations. Tragic divisions resulted. One outcome was the creation of many new "independent," "faith," and "direct-support" missionary societies to replace agencies that were no longer in essential subjection to the authority of Scripture.

In 1938, the International Missionary Conference again convened, this time at Tambaram, Madras. By now there had been some reaction, chiefly European in origin, against the humanism of Jerusalem. There was also a growing realization of the spiritual vigor and equality of the younger churches overseas. These latter brought the conference to recognize a biblically obvious, but often overlooked fact, namely: the Church itself is the "center and focal point of the whole missionary enterprise." The chief objective of missions is to plant churches. They in turn are to become centers of light for further missionary outreach. This was a positive note. Even evangelical missions were helped by this emphasis.

But at Tambaram the issue of theology again came to the fore, as a result of Dr. Hendrik Kraemer's pre-conference book, *The Christian Message in a Non-Christian World.*[9] Everyone was confronted with the problem of revelation, its nature and authority. True, Dr. Kraemer rejected the possibility of non-Christian faiths leading men to God or finding fulfillment in

9. London: Edinburgh House Press, 1938.

Christianity. This was a great improvement on Jerusalem. Evangelicals were encouraged. And yet, his dialectical approach to the Gospel records disturbed the evangelicals greatly. Was he separating Jesus of Nazareth from the Christ of God? Was not a measure of irrationality involved in minimizing the One while magnifying the Other? The Barthian dialectic was exerting a strong influence, and evangelicals were confused. The conference did not agree on theological matters, so its official releases were deliberately vague and inconclusive regarding all shades of conviction. It is significant that at these conferences the Holy Spirit was hardly even mentioned.[10]

After the agony and carnage of World War II, in which more than 50 million lost their lives, and the demonic aspect of man was uncovered as never before, a chastened convocation of leaders convened at Whitby, Canada, in 1947. No evangelical can take serious exception to the new vision granted those assembled for the evangelization of the world. The record of their deliberations reminds one of Edinburgh. The older Western churches confronted the younger churches, and frankly said, in as many words: "We accept you as our equals. Let us be partners-in-obedience for the

---

10. "One looks in vain for any real mention of the Holy Spirit in the Laymen's Inquiry or in *Rethinking Missions*. The index of Dr. Kraemer's work does not contain a single line on the Holy Spirit. In the seven volumes of the Madras Conference, almost every other subject is treated but not the Holy Spirit." Harold Lindsell, *Missionary Principles and Practice* (New York: Fleming H. Revell Company, 1955), p. 332.

evangelization of the world. What lead can you give us? What are your plans? How may we help you to discharge your evangelistic obligations?" Read their solid words:

> The Gospel is to be preached to all men. Can it be so preached in our generation? To preach to men is not the same as to convert them. God alone can command success, and it is always open to men to resist His will. Yet, when we consider the present extension of the Church, and the divine and human resources available, we dare to believe it possible that, before the present generation has passed away, the Gospel should be preached to almost all the inhabitants of the world in such a way as to make clear to them the issue of faith or disbelief in Jesus Christ. If this is possible it is the task of the Church to see that it is done.
>
> From the older churches the younger churches are asking for literally thousands of men and women as missionary helpers: to go into immense areas where the name of Christ has never been heard and where there is no hindrance to the preaching of the Gospel but the lack of a messenger; to take immediate advantage of opportunities in lands where it seems likely that the Gospel will not have free entry for more than another ten or fifteen years; to help in building up the Church in countries where thousands are being gathered in every year; to share in the training of leaders, up to the highest level, for theological, educational, social, medical and pastoral work.[11]

---

11. Charles W. Ransom (ed.), *Renewal and Advance* (London: Edinburgh House Press, 1948), pp. 215, 216.

125

The times were certainly against the implementation of the call issued at Whitby. Korea was soon engulfed in civil war, China in the throes of a communist take over, the subcontinent of India split by religious and social revolution, and the Muslim world in political reorganization. Subsequently, Whitby was largely disregarded as an impractical and idealistic conference. Basic theological issues were not faced. In any case, attention was soon diverted to Amsterdam, where the World Council of Churches was being formed (accomplished in 1948). The next International Missionary Conference, convened at Willingen, Germany, in 1952, was eclipsed by the growing strength of the World Council of Churches. Close observers noted that increasingly the old debate revolving around the theological basis of missions was coming to the fore. "What is the place of missions in the life and witness of the Church?" "What is the actual nature of the Church's mission?" These questions tended to push aside questions of strategy and advance. The International Missionary Council seemed to be bogging down in sterile debate and losing its sense of movement.

Then at Accra, Ghana, in 1957–58, a conference was convened that seemed to point an entirely new direction. "Why should there not be a joint assembly of the International Missionary Council and World Council of Churches, convened with a view to seeking an organizational integration of these two bodies? Why not eliminate the difference between churches and missions?

Why not a new concept: the Church is the Mission and the Mission is the Church? The day of missionary societies is over. Why not take aggressive steps toward the reunion of all the churches of Christendom, scattered throughout the earth?" These were the proposals which drew increasingly wide support.

In November 1961, at New Delhi, India, the movement toward integration was greatly accelerated—"the great forward step" of the Ecumenical Movement. Now the Ecumenical Movement has come to the fore. The World Council of Churches is emerging as the dominant body, even though it would never have gained its place in the sun had there not been the missionary movement with its long decades of growth and its international conventions. In a sense there is a great positive gain that has resulted from all this. For centuries missionary work has been done, almost in spite of the Church, rarely with its wholehearted blessing. A devoted, doggedly determined "remnant," never adequately supported with personnel and funds, has accomplished amazing deeds in planting the Church throughout the world. But now there appears to be the possibility of a great stimulus in evangelistic outreach by the whole Church throughout the whole world.

But the great, unresolved theological problems remain. It is here that the enlightened evangelical holds grave misgivings. In 1961, several months before the New Delhi Joint Assemblies of the International Missionary Council and the World Council of Churches, a significant book, already referred to in this chapter, was released: Gerald H. Anderson's *The Theology of the Christian Mission*.[12] Twenty-five of the leading contributors to current Protestant thought participated in an attempt, by reflection and debate, toward "the building of a new theological edifice for the Christian Mission in today's world." Tillich, Barth, Bouquet, Cullmann, DeWolf, Kraemer, Warren, and Hogg are among the authors. Significantly, the book's subject was the key item on the New Delhi agenda.

The book reflects the spread of opinion and the various areas of agreement and disagreement that characterize the Ecumenical Movement today. The grave issues that divided churches at home and their missions overseas in the 1930's are still present. The current debate within the World Council of Churches on the basic problem of finding theological justification for presenting the Christian gospel to devotees of non-Christian religions is moving away steadily from the historic evangelical position.

Some Dominant Characteristics

The vast literature of the Ecumenical Movement today strikes certain major chords almost constantly. It is characterized by features which include the following.

12. The quotations on the next few pages are from this book. The page numbers are incorporated in the text for easier reference.

1. *Inclusivist message*

One must share with Dr. Kraemer his long-standing sense of indignation with the Ecumenical Movement because of its unwillingness to take "practical measures to combat syncretism" within its ranks. There is no other possible reaction for the evangelical to make to the allegation that the early Christians "may have been over-zealous" in affirming that "there is no other name given under heaven" for the salvation of men (F. H. Ross, p. 219). No evangelical can sympathize with the view that "all of the early Christians' affirmations about Jesus the Christ were in the mythic dimension." This claim is expounded as follows: "They believed that Christ was in some sense the 'Messiah,' or the 'son of Man' or 'Son of God.' Some believed that He had a 'virgin birth.' All of these themes are ancient mythic themes, paralleled over and over again in the religions of mankind" (p. 221). One is reminded of *Rethinking Missions* when he reads: "Faith is not bound by any particular system of dogmas or ideas. . . . As man's free response to the divine act it has the freedom to choose between various doctrines, ideas and cultural patterns so that it may be able to create a new system of doctrines and ideas" (Masatoshi Doi, p. 177).

Not all the contributors to Anderson's book are religious relativists. There are those leaders in the movement who are unequivocally Christian in the New Testament sense, holding to what others label an "Only Way rigidity." Yet, they remain in the movement. They have undoubtedly felt the risks of participating worth taking, and have done so with honest convictions. These have probably been influenced by the example of evangelicals in the Church of England who rejoice that historic, biblical Christianity has a significant place in their communion, even though the total Anglican theological spectrum ranges from Roman sacramentalism to practical Unitarianism. They are likewise aware that vital biblical Christianity in Britain diminished in those groups (Methodist, Baptist, Congregational) which in past years withdrew from the Church of England for theological reasons. They not unnaturally hope that by reunion these groups will come into contact with New Testament Christianity once again.

2. *Uncertain missionary outreach*

What attitude would one take toward the non-Christian religions? For the evangelical, the Scriptures speak clearly. They affirm again and again that the Christian message is not only unique, but also exclusive.

Within the Ecumenical Movement the issue is uncertain. Some hold that Christianity has an "absoluteness" about its essential elements. Others see in Christianity something neither final nor suited to all mankind. Their viewpoint is as follows: Since there is "the good in all religions," Christianity in its ultimate

130

form, as it unfolds from the reconciliation and reunion of all Christendom, will then become the fulfillment of all heathen religions. There is no such thing as a doctrinal Christianity, no finality to Jesus of Nazareth, and no need for evangelizing the Jews and Gentiles in the New Testament pattern. "Jesus promises that even those who have never heard of Him, heathen and non-Christians, who to their own surprise turn out to be Christians because they have fulfilled the command of love, will be received into the Kingdom of God and will sit at table there with Him. . . . The criterion which determines the consignment of men to the kingdom of God or to outer darkness is not a definite doctrine about Christ, not a recognition of the Christian claim to absoluteness, nor is it even a knowledge of the historical figure of Jesus" (Ernest Benz, pp. 143–144).

It is argued that the times are so dark, the growth of secularism so rapid, that "Christians should seriously heed" the call to "inter-religious cooperation" overseas. The Ecumenical Movement virtually calls on the individual Christian to surrender his distinctiveness and work with all and sundry who are laboring to maintain the religious dimension in modern life! This is a far cry from the evangelical call to rescue by the gospel those who are doomed to eternal punishment, to "everlasting destruction from the presence of the Lord." Yet such rigidity of viewpoint, Tillich comments, is "unworthy of the glory and of the love of God and must be rejected in the name of the true relationship of God to His world" (Paul Tillich, pp. 283–284).

The evangelical cannot accept this devitalized, humanistic Christianity that sees neither centrality in Jesus Christ nor eternal salvation for mankind solely through His Cross. It matters little how popular, how persuasive, how powerful this movement becomes if it is not being guided by basic biblical principles. In fact, the authoritative Word which is Christ himself, and the ancient Jewish Scriptures He trusted, obeyed, and promised to supplement with a New Covenant, are slavishly subordinated to human reason. The Ecumenical Movement currently appears to be more of man than of God. As such, how can it but fail?

3. *Aggressive organizational outreach*

In recent years a new sequence of organizational patterns within Protestantism has been unfolding with mounting speed. For many years—perhaps too many—administrative control on the field was in the hands of the foreign missionaries and their governing boards in the homelands. As the national churches emerged and grew, however, national leaders began to share in field administration. Eventually these churches were organized into separate national councils, in which both missionaries and nationals participated. But with the growth of nationalism, it became apparent that missionaries should take a back seat and grant national churches full autonomy. This generally resulted in the establishment of an over-all National Christian Council, in which the churches brought into being by the various missions were further united, with missionary societies excluded and foreign missionaries only serving in advisory capacities. These have eventually been transformed organizationally into a centralized "Church of Christ" for the whole nation. Because of the inclusivist theological beliefs of the leadership of these national churches, as well as their historic orientation to the old-line denominations, these national churches have tended to by-pass evangelical churches and missions. Ironically, the latter's spiritual contribution and outreach more often than not exceeded that represented by the united "Church of Christ." It is these separate national "Churches of Christ" that have been so intimately related to the International Missionary Council.

A recent study released by the Staff Council of the Division of Foreign Missions of the National Christian Council of Churches in America has detailed the strategy for advance in East Asia. Its pattern is representative of the organizational drive taking place within the Ecumenical Movement today.

(a) Strengthen the National Christian Councils in each country until these Councils are strong enough to win the support of the local churches and to furnish leadership for the Christian movement in each country.

133

(b) Enlist groups that are not ready for full co-operation in the National Christian Councils in special parts of the program, such as literacy, audio-visual and radio, Christian literature, and relief.

(c) Organize strategy committees in connection with the National Christian Councils and help new missions find their place in an area with the best comity arrangements.

(d) Keep strong united churches within the framework of the National Christian Councils so that there can be cooperation of the strong and the weaker churches for nation-wide projects.[13]

A good example of the implementation of the movement's strategy can be observed in Vietnam. The Evangelical Church of Vietnam, a fully self-supporting national church that is largely the result of the faithful labors of the Christian and Missionary Alliance, has been approached by the International Missionary Council's Inter-Church Aid program with a tempting offer. The program offered to subsidize pastors, provide capital funds and professors for a theological seminary, make financially possible the participation of Vietnamese pastors and Youth Teams in promotional tours throughout Southeast Asia on behalf of inter-church fellowship, and set up a scholarship fund to enable college-age students to study overseas. This intrusion

---

13. *Some Statements on Cooperation,* Committee on Research in Foreign Missions, February 18, 1952, p. 5.

has been protested, but these persuasive pressures have not been withdrawn.

An Evangelical Evaluation

What is to be the response of the evangelical Christian to the Ecumenical Movement? Biblical principles are our only guide if we are to evaluate this complex problem with any degree of accuracy. The following key areas should be considered.

1. *Union*

For Christians to be divided is a "scandal and a shame." But the problem of disunity is not new. Even in Christ's day, there was an occasion when His disciples came upon a stranger casting out demons in His name, and forbade him on the ground that "he followeth not with us." But Christ rebuked them. "Forbid him not," He said, "for he that is not against us is for us" (Luke 9:49–50).

Down through its twenty centuries of history, the Christian church has never been united in an institutional sense. But despite this, it is the will of our Lord that His people be united in such a way "that the world may believe . . . and . . . know" that He is the sent One of God (John 17:21, 23). Great texts in Scripture affirm the need of Christians for one another, because they are already spiritually united in Christ their Head. ". . . keep the unity of the Spirit. . . . Till we all come in the unity of the faith, and of the

135

knowledge of the Son of God . . ." (Ephesians 4:3, 13). Growth in faith and knowledge depends on the experiential unity and interaction of God's people in Christ around His Word.

The Ecumenical Movement is thoroughly biblical when it affirms that Christians are members of One Body, even Christ's very own, and that Christians share a common fellowship with Christ in His Church. Preoccupation with preaching the gospel and winning men to Christ is not enough. Visible churches must be planted that are in vital fellowship with others "of like precious faith." Disunity in the name of Christ is indeed a scandal.

No responsible Christian can approve on biblical grounds the "Christian cannibalism" frequently displayed by some evangelicals today: "Ye bite and devour one another, take heed that ye be not consumed one of another" (Gal. 5:15). We need one another. When we live in isolation from one another, it only results in our spiritual impoverishment. Let us no longer be afraid of one another. True, in coming together, we may be obliged to surrender some of our pet ideas and individual independence. But the unity of a man and woman in marriage involves a similar sharing and surrender. No one will deny that enrichment and wholeness is the happy result.

The unity Christ yearns for us to keep is not to be sought merely for the sake of outward show. His concern is for a unity based upon spiritual reality, not unlike the union of the Father and the Son (John 17:11). It is a unity based on truth and the possession of a common life. It is the result of a surrender of the entire being to the Lord (John 1:12) and to one another in the fear of God (Eph. 5:21). If there is an issue between organizational unity and truth, the truth must be obeyed. This does not mean, however, that one should allow loyalty to minor matters of interpretation to prevent one from entering experientially into vital fellowship with his Christian brethren. Nothing is more absurd and pathetic in certain evangelical circles today than the practice of excluding from our fellowship those whom we cannot agree with on minute details of eschatology.

And yet, the Scriptures are unequivocal in their insistence that there must be agreement on essential truths. "He who is of God hears the words of God; the reason why you do not hear them is that you are not of God" (John 8:47). "There is . . . one Lord, one faith, one baptism" (Ephesians 4:4, 5). ". . . complete my joy by being of the same mind, having the same love, being in full accord and of one mind. . . . Have this mind among yourselves, which you have in Christ Jesus" (Philippians 2:2, 5). "Any one who goes ahead and does not abide in the doctrine of Christ does not have God; he who abides in the doctrine of Christ has both the Father and the Son. If any one comes to you and does not bring this doctrine, do not receive him into the house or give him greetings; for he who

137

greets him shares his wicked work" (II John 9–11), etc. In the Ecumenical Movement today Scriptures such as these are largely overlooked. While one laments the scandal and shame of the disunity of the Church, he is also obliged to confess that an even greater scandal and shame is the disloyalty of the Church to Jesus Christ and His Word. His person and work are often minimized, His view of the Old Testament widely scorned. His exclusive concept of salvation is largely dismissed.

2. *Discipline*

The New Testament has a great deal to say about Church discipline, defining its underlying principles and illustrating their application from the lives and ministry of the apostles. Everything is ultimately based on the instruction of Christ himself. How frequently He warned against those who proclaimed error. "Beware of false prophets, which come to you in sheep's clothing, but inwardly they are ravening wolves" (Matt. 7:15). "Many false prophets shall rise, and shall deceive many" (Matt. 24:11), etc. In similar vein the Apostle Paul speaks of sound doctrine—that which is necessary to salvation—and warns of the time when men will no longer endure it. He even refers to religious teaching that may be the "doctrines of demons" (I Timothy 4:1, 6, 11, 16; 6:3; II Timothy 4:3, 4, etc.). Indifference to doctrine per se could almost be classifiable as indifference to Jesus Christ!

In contrast, the Ecumenical Movement holds that

"Doctrine separates but service unites." By this affirmation it renders impossible any protection of "the purity of the Church." This greatly disturbs evangelicals because of their sense of history and their awareness that the Scriptures distinctly teach that the period just prior to the glorious return of Christ will witness a widespread apostasy from the "faith once delivered." History records how the Church has departed from the faith again and again in the past. Moreover, the Bible teaches how in the future, during the "end time," there will emerge a vast religious system that will claim to be Christ's true Church but will be terribly false! If the Ecumenical system regards discipline on doctrinal grounds as behind the times, one cannot exclude the possibility of its finding tragic eschatological fulfillment in that adulterous woman, "Mystery Babylon," portrayed in Revelation 17.

3. *Separation*

Scripture teaches that God's people will always find this world a hostile environment for true discipleship. There is always the possibility of defilement and defeat. Unregenerate man in his rebellion against God, his unconscious slavery to his own self-centered nature, and his exposure to the blinding blandishments of the "god of this world," has always been basically hostile toward all those who have been called by God's grace (John 15:19). Scripture is filled with the record of the constant tension existing between the world and the

139

man of God. The desire to preserve a pure testimony and live a godly life is always challenged, from within and from without.

In order that His own might overcome, God has decreed the principle of separation. It is unfolded from Genesis to Revelation. To cite texts is almost superfluous, they are so extensive in number and pointed in meaning (II Corinthians 6:14, 15; Galatians 1:8; II Thessalonians 3:6; I Timothy 6:3–5; II Timothy 3:5; II John 9–11, drawn from the New Testament alone). There are rival Gods, separate from them. There are rival Christs, separate from them. There are false gospels, separate from them. "Let us go forth therefore unto him [Christ] without the camp, bearing his reproach. For here have we no continuing city, but we seek one to come" (Hebrews 13:13, 14)

Much of the Old Testament is taken up with the melancholy record of the consequences that come to individuals and nations when they disobey the Word of God by failing to separate themselves unto the Lord and from the world. Unfortunately, in our day among evangelicals there have been such violations of much that Scripture says regarding the Law of Love and the sacredness of truth, such uncrucified pride, and such unnecessary divisions within the visible Church—all in the name of "separation"—that the underlying biblical truth of this matter has been largely discredited and ignored. Certainly, "an enemy hath done this."

Church history likewise is replete with multiple evidence of the validity of this great principle. But the Ecumenical Movement, by its very inclusivist nature, makes loyalty in this area not only suspect, but virtually impossible. This disregard for the hard lessons of Scripture, reinforced by the awful confirmations of Church history, is sufficient to give the reflective evangelical some sorrowful moments as he watches the onward march of this movement.

Conclusion

The question arises: How does this affect the Church throughout the world? Fortunately, on the overseas mission fields, the percentage of nationals who are evangelical is considerably higher than in the Church in the homelands. More than half of the world missionary task force (as we have already recorded) is likewise evangelical in conviction. Anyone who has traveled widely in mission field areas cannot easily forget the evidence of what God has wrought through the faithful few. The "good seed" has been widely scattered.

Is the solution of this whole tangle to be found in organizing parallel councils, national churches, and world fellowships? Some feel this to be the answer. The World Evangelical Fellowship currently has 23 participating national fellowships. The International Christian Council of Churches likewise claims a worldwide following. When one is at the grassroots level of these organizations, however, he finds they have not deeply penetrated the hearts and captured the imaginations of national Christians overseas. They are too closely identified with American cultural imperialism, too American-controlled, too American-financed, and as a result too emotionally involved in the ideological East-West conflict of these times. Some are hopeful that the British-oriented World Evangelical Alliance will temper the World Evangelical Fellowship, with which it is associated.

To be positive, evangelicals today should affirm their concern for the disunity existing among the Lord's people. Concurrently they should guard against any easy optimism that sees the whole matter of unity realized through the erection of a finely balanced organization to which all groupings, church and mission, are pressed to join.

A far deeper concern for the "unity of the faith, and of the knowledge of the Son of God" is called for. Christians should meet together and enter into dialogue with one another. We should work together whenever the opportunity presents, that the world may hear the gospel and believe on the One whom God has sent to be its Lord and Savior.

Such efforts as "Evangelism in Depth" sparked by the Latin America Mission have stirred the imagination of many concerned about the disunity of the Church and the millions as yet unreached. First in Nicaragua and later in Costa Rica, all the Christians— nationals and foreign missionaries (denominational and non-denominational)—have joined forces month

142

after month to reach their nations for Christ. The ties that united them in the Lord were discovered to be far stronger than the minor issues that formerly caused them to follow separate paths. This newly realized spiritual unity has revealed tremendous potential. It needs to be consolidated and expanded. It may well prove God's means in other countries where national churches exist and yet remain divided.

But what of the future? The future course of the Ecumenical Movement is not clear. Perhaps this is because it is too man-oriented. After all, the Church is Christ's. He is its Lord and Redeemer. And we dare not forget that He said, "I will build my Church; and the gates of hell shall not prevail against it."

This brings us to the only worthy center of the focus. Jesus Christ lives in the midst of His Church. There shall come a day when a completed, cleansed, and glorified Church shall be with Him. Then every knee shall bow to Him, and every tongue shall confess His pre-eminence and glory. The present may be confused, the future uncertain. But let us rest in God's ultimate triumph.

Amen! Even so come, Lord Jesus!

Part III. The Church on the Offensive

Chapter 7: **Meeting Racism Head-on**

T HE EARLY JEWISH APOSTLES found it extraordinarily difficult to realize that other nations beside their own had a significant role to play in the universal purpose of God. The same problem of cultural and national narrow-mindedness is with us today.

Some Historical Considerations

The increase in the apostles' understanding of God's purpose following the outpouring of the Holy Spirit at Pentecost was quite remarkable. There is an astounding contrast between the question in the first chapter of the Acts, ". . . Lord, will you at this time restore the kingdom to Israel?" (verse 6), which revealed that even at that late date they were looking for an earthly Jewish kingdom, and the truth expressed by Peter, "For the promise is to you and to your children and to all that are far off, every one whom the Lord our God calls to him" (Acts 2:39).

In the light of this revelation, and the fact that before

147

His ascension Jesus had repeatedly explained the world-wide scope of His plan and commission, it seems strange that the apostles were so reluctant to shed their cultural and mental insularity. That they were reluctant is clearly indicated in Acts 10 by the painstaking way the Lord broke down the prejudice of Peter and brought him to a place where he was willing to preach to Cornelius, a Roman centurion. Their insularity is also manifested in the nineteenth verse of Acts 11, "Now those who were scattered because of the persecution that arose over Stephen traveled as far as Phoenicia and Cyprus and Antioch, *speaking the word to none except Jews.*" Thus we may note that although the gospel spread rapidly, it took some time before it burst out of the Jewish culture in which the Church had been born.

For the first two-and-a-half centuries of its exist-ence, the Church suffered bitter persecution, with only brief respite, at the hands of imperial Rome. It is un-derstandable, but inexpressibly sad, that when the policy of the Roman Empire changed so that it first tolerated and then courted the Church, the latter re-sponded with such uncritical enthusiasm that she be-came more obviously the bride of the Roman Caesar than the bride of Christ. The Church became so closely identified with the power, politics, and culture of imperial Rome that when that empire was eventually crushed, the Church was seriously shattered, surviving with very little prestige and even less spiritual power. "Those who do not remember the past," wrote the philosopher George Santayana, "are condemned to re-live it." The Church should take note.

The manner in which God deals with nations, as with individuals, is an awesome study and a revealing one. God overrules in the affairs of the nations. It is no coincidence that the most rapid recent expansion of the Church coincided with periods when Britain and later the United States exercised a pre-eminent posi-tion in world affairs. The winds of their economic and political prosperity enabled the seeds of the gospel to be spread worldwide. But the Church failed to learn from history; again and again, she allowed herself to become far too closely identified with the white man and his sometimes oppressive colonial policies. The charge that missionaries were "tools of the imperialists" was not entirely without foundation; for consciously or not, the Church contributed actively in the struggle of capitalistic nations for world power.

It is interesting to note comments on this subject from the Soviet Press: for instance, the following ex-cerpt from an article on missions in the *Great Soviet Encyclopedia*, 2d ed., Vol. 27, as translated by Dr. Donald A. Lowrie.

At the end of the 18th century great Protestant mis-sionary organizations arose. . . . Their activities adopted more clever and refined forms (the organiza-tion of schools, libraries, children's homes, hospitals, etc.). Missionary activities played an active role in the struggle of the capitalistic countries for the division

149

of the world into zones of influence and for plundering the colonies. As agents of the capitalist states, the missionaries lived under the protection of these states, received from them subsidies and all sorts of privileges. The unjust Tientsin Treaty which was forced upon China in 1858 provided among other things, special privileges for missionaries. The rising of the popular masses in colonial and dependent countries against the foreign yoke was directed against the missionaries as well.

Time was when a white skin was sufficient to guarantee a respectful hearing of the gospel. In an age of colonialism, it was difficult to avoid some overtones of paternalism creeping into the Church. Nevertheless, it is hard to excuse such a spirit and relationship in the light of the example and instructions of the Founder of the Church, who "came not to be served but to serve," and of His great missionary apostle, who owed much of his success to the fact that he was prepared to be "your servant for Jesus' sake."

The day of the white man's undisputed supremacy is over. This has taken place partly by sheer human multiplication. While the population of Europe is expanding at the annual rate of only 0.8 per cent and that of North America expanding at 1.7 per cent, the rate of expansion for Central America is 2.7 per cent, for South America 2.4 per cent, and for Southwest Asia 2.5 per cent.[1] This revolutionary change in the uni-

1. Richard M. Fagley, *The Population Explosion and Christian Responsibility* (New York: Oxford University Press, 1960), p. 23.

versal social order, largely stemming from the population explosion, has been accelerated by a tremendous
advance in education and by political changes of unforeseen magnitude. For generations Afro-Asians were
prepared to accept domination by the white man. They
had little alternative or incentive to do otherwise. But
today the colored peoples of the earth sense the arrival
of a new day of freedom and opportunity. Coupled with
this sense of destiny is a profound disillusionment with
the white man. In commenting on the pressures within
the British Commonwealth that forced South Africa
to withdraw from its ranks, *The Economist* comments:
"Black and brown countries already make up nearly
seven-eighths of the Commonwealth's population, and
as more Afro-Asians join the club, their Prime Ministers are going to make the Queen look like a white dot
in a dark sea when they have their photograph taken at
their annual meeting. . . . What is astonishing when
one looks back on it is that the non-white countries of
the Commonwealth should have waited so patiently
and so long before they flexed their muscles against
South Africa's racial policy." [2]

No Christian should deplore the disappearance of the
myth of white superiority. Unfortunately, however,
it is not merely the white man's policies that have been
repudiated, but often his religion also; for to millions
in the world today, Christianity is "the white man's

---

2. *The Economist*, March 25, 1961, page 1160.

religion." This is tragic irony for a religion that was born in the East and less than three hundred miles west of the line of longitude that saw the birthplace of Islam.

Some Biblical Principles

When God chose the Jewish nation to be the womb of the Church, He chose a people of great exclusiveness. Yet the very circumstances surrounding the birth of the Church—a gathering of people from many nations, the authentication of the event by a supernatural diversity of tongues—gave dramatic evidence that it was His will that the Church should be multiracial. Soon the nerve center of the Church changed from Jerusalem to Antioch, and from that cosmopolitan city the Church's influence radiated to every corner of the Roman Empire. Thus in writing to the Christians at Ephesus, the Apostle Paul described as one of the wonderful results of the death of Christ His destruction of the centuries-old wall of hostility between Jew and Gentile.

Therefore remember that at one time you Gentiles . . . were at that time separated from Christ, alienated from the commonwealth of Israel, and strangers to the covenants of promise, having no hope and without God in the world. But now in Christ Jesus you who once were far off have been brought near in the blood of Christ. For he is our peace, who has made us both one, and has broken down the dividing wall of hostility, by abolishing in his flesh the law of commandments and ordinances, that he might create in himself one new man in place of the two, so making peace, and might reconcile us both to God in one body through the cross, thereby bringing the hostility to an end. And he came and preached peace to you who were far off and peace to those who were near; for through him we both have access in one Spirit to the Father (Ephesians 2:11–18).

The huge resources of the Church in North America place upon that Church a solemn responsibility for a large share in the evangelization of the world. But scriptural principles and today's situation demand vigorous thought and humble self-criticism, combined with courageous action to break through the Anglo-Saxon dominance of the Church and to stress the multiracial and supranational character of the Church of Jesus Christ.

Basically this is a spiritual matter. Pride of race and culture are far more deeply ingrained in us than we imagine, and this pride must be crucified. Our allegiance to God and His kingdom impose an incomparably higher loyalty than that which binds us to family, race, or nationality. When God decided to create a people for himself, He called Abraham, who was immediately faced with a conflict of interests. "Go from your country, and your kindred and your father's house to the land that I will show you" (Genesis 12:1). Jesus Christ applied this principle to Christian discipleship when He said, "He who loves father or mother more than me is not worthy of me; and he who loves son or daughter more than me is not worthy of me; and he who does not take his cross and follow me is not worthy of me" (Matthew 13:37, 38). One may accept this principle intellectually, but stumble over it emotionally when trying to put it into practice. Disagreement in a local church often reveals how few can rise above family loyalties and affections. Many Christians in the United States and elsewhere, who are firmly persuaded of the rightness of integration, have mixed feelings when it comes to implementing integration practically in church membership and community affairs. The immobility and strict silence of many evangelicals since the 1954 Supreme Court decision on school integration may well have indirectly aided the efforts of extremists such as the Ku Klux Klan. If the Christian community does not care sufficiently to act individually, then apparently other less pious people such as the freedom riders, few of whom are Christians, will.

Luther's anti-Semitism, the disastrous consequences of which have already been noted, has more than one contemporary counterpart. The nationalist policy of "apartheid" as enforced in South Africa, though technically calculated to maintain apartness, in fact imposes white racial supremacy on a dictatorial basis, and has drawn some of its heaviest support from the Dutch Reformed Church of South Africa. Moreover, the timidity and vacillation of some evangelicals and their frequent refusal to state the true scriptural teaching have helped to discredit Christianity in the eyes of the African. The

154

full harvest of apartheid has yet to be reaped, and the Church has largely herself to blame if she suffers a bloody nose, if not a fiery trial of faith.

Some Practical Suggestions

In addition to the application of biblical principles there are some very practical steps that can be taken to increase the role of the non-Caucasian.

1. *Enlarging the contribution of the American non-Caucasian.* Judson is generally regarded as the pioneer of United States foreign missions. Few people are aware that in 1783, thirty years before Judson sailed for Burma, a liberated American Negro left this country as a missionary for Jamaica. The work of this former slave was so successful that by 1842, the church he had established was responsible for forty-five missionaries serving in Africa.

More than a century later the following extract is illuminating:

James T. Robinson, a negro, found his skin color to be a great asset as he traveled in many parts of the world. He states, "On a recent mission to students around the world for the Board of Foreign Missions of the Presbyterian Church U.S.A. I spent the largest bulk of my time in Asia. For once in my life the color of my skin and the accident of my race as an American negro were assets rather than handicaps. Every door was open to me. In fact, I went many places where white people are no longer welcome. Very often an Asian government official would offer me a seat and

155

leave my white missionary companion standing. Non-Christians of all the other religions seemed as anxious to open their hearts and doors to me as did the Christian nationals who had been won by the missionary enterprise. In Southwest India some Moslems left their service in a mosque on a Friday night and came instead into a Christian church where I was preaching. When I asked one of them why, he said, 'You are the first American we have ever seen who looks like us and you were saying the things in which we are interested. You have suffered as we have and you can understand us. We can talk to you as we can never talk to white Americans.' No question was more consistently and pointedly asked me than, 'Why don't you send us negro missionaries?' " [3]

No one should underestimate the difficulties and dangers in the use of Negroes as missionaries. There is always the possibility that the Negro missionary, when corrected for perfectly normal shortcomings, will feel he is the victim of racial persecution. There is the difficulty of disparity between the standard of living of the American Negro missionary and the national pastors among whom he works and whom he frequently resembles facially. Much is being made of the problem of intermarriage with white missionaries. Also, there are a few countries where even visas for Negroes would be difficult to get. But anyone closely identified with the missionary cause will recognize that comparable prob-

---

3. Calvin Lewis Roesler, *The American Negro as a Foreign Missionary* (Master's Thesis, Columbia Bible College, 1953).

lems are involved in sending out white missionaries. Almost everything depends upon the careful screening and preparation of candidates before they leave their home country. A number of mission boards have recently reported enthusiastically their fruitful experience in the use of American Negroes for missionary service overseas. It is an extremely encouraging sign, too, that many more mission boards are willing to accept such missionaries than would have been the case, say, ten years ago. Indeed, it should be noted that present openings for Negro missionaries are far in excess of the number of recruits. Owing to the nature of Negro churches and the pathetic state of Negro education, both secular and Christian, for which the white population must share the blame, there are very few potential candidates for the mission field. But there is still plenty of room for imagination and innovation on the part of missionary agencies in the use of the American Negro if his full potential is to be realized.

Although drawn from a different national and cultural background, the reservoir of Negroes in the British West Indies Federation has been virtually untapped. The many flourishing Negro churches here have recently seen an enlarging of overseas missionary interest among their students. It is to be hoped that this interest will prove fruitful.

Much of what has been written concerning the American Negro applies also to the American citizen of Oriental descent. Such a person working in the

157

Orient has some very decided advantages, but equally some definite difficulties to face. A missionary recently remarked that the nisei (an American-born citizen of Japanese descent) who is not Japanese-speaking has nevertheless usually had sufficient exposure to the language to enable him to learn Japanese when he arrives in Japan far more readily than an American white missionary. But a nisei, who had just finished one tour of service in Japan and was preparing to return, commented that a man who looks Japanese and has a Japanese name, but who acts and thinks like an American, is far more unpopular with the Japanese than an American of Anglo-Saxon descent. When asked how many nisei had made a satisfactory adaptation to the Japanese culture, he commented that out of forty or fifty whom he had known in Japan, only six, he felt, had really succeeded in identifying themselves with the Japanese and their way of life.

It would seem that with some splendid exceptions, mission boards have been more reluctant to accept Orientals than Negroes; some evangelical mission boards have been slow to accept either. Often this has been due less to a definite policy of refusing such applicants than to a habit of simply making it difficult for them to be accepted. It is untrue to say that the world awaits the mobilization of American non-Caucasians for world evangelization; for the Negro churches and the oriental churches within the United States themselves need the revitalizing that manifests itself in a real missionary vision and outreach.

2. *Stimulating missionary vision in younger churches.* Throughout the world many churches, established by missionaries, have been on the receiving end for so long that they have very little concept of their responsibility and privilege of contributing to the evangelization of the world. This is very largely an indictment of the Western missionary enterprise rather than of individual churches. There are bright spots, however, which only serve to accentuate the extent of our failure. For instance, a great and growing church has been established in Latin America that has witnessed exciting developments in the last twenty-five years. In most countries, however, it seems that Christians have very little sense of responsibility for the unreached tribes of their own countries, much less the unreached millions of other continents. To impart a missionary vision to any church requires first and foremost a heart of love for Jesus Christ; second, a more intensive system of missionary education. The Church could do a great deal more to foster such a vision in the younger churches throughout the world.

3. *Utilizing international teams.* Certain mission boards throughout the world have made it a policy to segregate missionaries of various nationalities, allocating one section of a particular country to, for instance, British missionaries, and another section of the same

159

country to American missionaries. If there were ever a time when such insularity was justified, it is certainly unpardonable today. In stressing the supranational quality of the Church, it is of inestimable value to create teams comprised of diverse nationalities and backgrounds, and, when at all possible, to place them under leadership of non-Caucasians.

4. *Providing partnership status in mission boards.* In implementing the international aspect of the Church of Jesus Christ, there are some boards which have followed a policy of taking nationals resident in a country and making them members of an American mission board. This is, of course, much more readily accomplished when the nationals concerned are culturally closer to North America; for example, such a program is easier to implement in Latin American countries with well-educated Latin Americans than with primitive Indians.

How practical this policy may be in each instance may be questioned, and much discussion and even controversy has centered around the issue. We must encourage, however, every honest attempt to stress the international aspect of the missionary enterprise consistent with over-all biblical principles.

5. *Using American funds wisely.* God has bountifully blessed North America, so that her capacity to contribute to world evangelism in material as well as human resources outweighs that of any other continent. But these finances need to be dispensed with great wis-

dom and care, and, as far as possible, should be pooled with the resources of other countries. Thus the origin of the finances in use becomes less obvious and tends much less toward the subordination of the interests and independence of the Church outside of North America.

In years ahead, if we still have years in which to accomplish our task, the Church must rapidly mobilize her full resources. This will certainly include the non-Caucasian—unless we permit our race prejudice, and our poverty of imagination and faith, to kill his potential contribution. It may well be that, when the history of the Church is finally written, the next decade may be called the day of the non-Caucasian.

Chapter 8: **Rethinking the Nonprofessional's Role**

T**HE MISSIONARY PURPOSE** of God embraces preaching the gospel to every creature and planting the Church in every culture. By this means He will gather out of the nations an eternal people for His name.

The task is vast and complex. The Scriptures must be translated, and the grace of God in Christ proclaimed in every language. Converts must be established in patterns of personal discipleship and group dynamics until vigorous local congregations result. The goal for these churches is that they should represent a threefold integration between the written Word of God, the life of Christ within the Christians, and the separate culture in which they live, refined and renewed by the Holy Spirit. This involves not deculturalizing men, much less Westernizing them, but rather permitting the distinctivenesses of all peoples to be brought into the heavenly Zion. Finally, these indigenous churches must

162

likewise participate in the missionary purpose of God, crossing cultural frontiers for the Lord's sake.

Two Methods, Not One

In order to accomplish this purpose God has ordained two distinct methods. These are clearly described in Acts, and the history of the Church is replete with evidence of their use, from the time of the apostles onward. They are summed up today in the terms "professional" and "nonprofessional" missionary methods. They should be studied carefully and thoroughly understood. Both are valid and God-given. Both enjoy His blessing. God deals with His people as individuals and as congregations that they might utilize these two methods throughout the earth. His immediate concern is that those whom He leads to use one method should not compete with, or criticize, those whom He leads to use the other. After all, it is He alone who gives the increase. The multiple evidence of the use of these two methods reveals the "one and the same Spirit, dividing to each [man] in particular according as He pleases" (I Corinthians 12:11, Darby).

At the very time when a vast body of missionaries were being withdrawn from the Congo, UNESCO appealed for 300 salaried teachers to man the Congo schools. Only 131 volunteered, and there was not one American among them. Without ignoring the formidable difficulties facing a teacher in Congo, one would conclude that a core of well-trained and spiritually effective teachers could have exercised a powerful influence for Christ, even though conventional missionaries had been withdrawn from that troubled land.

The number of Americans going abroad has increased tremendously in the last decade. In the year 1947, there were 435,000 who spent some time abroad. By 1957 there were 1,500,000. These Americans-away-from-home exert undoubted influence; certainly, the relations between the United States and the rest of the world are deeply affected by their character, training, and behavior.

In summary, there were more than 100,000 American civilians working abroad on a full-time basis for international organizations in 1956, approximately divided as follows:

United States Government and Government Contracts	37,000
Religious Missionary Organizations	28,000
American Business Enterprises	24,000
Students	10,000
Teachers and Scholars	1,500
International Organizations and Agencies	3,000
Voluntary Agencies and Philanthropic Foundations	1,000

In addition there were probably another 30,000 United States citizens who went abroad on short-term private or government business.

To these figures might be added the unknown number of Americans who work directly for a foreign government or a foreign business or who are self-employed in

164

foreign countries. For the purpose of emphasizing the problem of education and training for civilians in service overseas, the one million American troops stationed outside the continental limits of the United States have not even been listed. And *none of the figures include the wives or dependents* of personnel at work abroad.[1]

Much attention has been drawn to the Peace Corps of the Kennedy Administration. The idea of young people serving selflessly in various parts of the world in their respective professions and skills has received much publicity. Few seem to be aware that the Church has had its peace corps for many, many years. Medical doctors, engineers, school teachers, university professors, agriculturists, and business men have been using their specialized skills to serve the Lord in Afghanistan and Zanzibar, Africa and Latin America, Europe and Southeast Asia.

The Nonprofessional Ministry

What is a nonprofessional missionary or a vocational missionary as he is sometimes called? Neither term is wholly desirable. To use the phrase "nonprofessional" is to refer to the more usual type of missionary as a "professional"—which has certain unpleasant connotations in the minds of some. To avoid this the phrase "vocational missionary" has been coined. But this is even more misleading, as by inference it gives

1. Gerard J. Mangone, "Dungaree and Grey-Flannel Diplomacy," *The Art of Overseasmanship*, ed. Harlan Cleveland and Gerard J. Mangone (Syracuse: Syracuse University Press, 1957), pp. 12, 27.

the impression that the missionary working with the mission board does not have a vocation; moreover, the "nonprofessional" missionary may be confused with vocational men and women who are working with mission boards—i.e., agriculturists, medical technicians, etc. In the absence of a better term, we shall use that of "nonprofessional" missionary in this chapter.

By this term we mean a person who does not receive salary from a mission board or church and is not subject to the discipline of a mission board, but who travels abroad to aid in the mission of the Church and who supports himself by his own skill and labor.

Some have suggested that such a missionary is the only one that can operate successfully in the world of today. Others feel that the whole idea is an unmitigated nuisance which, in offering a higher standard of living than do most mission boards, tends to attract young people away from the more traditional service. In reality neither view is quite accurate. We do not have to choose between one or the other; we need both. "Nonprofessional" missionary work offers some important advantages. It also suffers from some severe drawbacks.

Advantages

The "nonprofessional" is never a financial burden on the church. Whether he be paid by UNESCO, a national government, or a private business, the expense of his travel, work, food, etc., is not paid by the church. An important fact to bear in mind is that the bill for

Protestant mission boards in North America mounted to almost $170,000,000 in 1959.[3]

This constitutes more than an economic advantage. The "nonprofessional" has a ready reply to those who gibe, "You preach because you are paid to preach." Moreover, there are many national Christians who have never met an American Christian who was not paid to preach. This example can be invaluable to them, particularly as one of the curses of the modern-day church is "professionalism."

The "nonprofessional" enjoys further advantages. For example, because of his work, he may find himself in contact with classes of people rarely touched by the ordinary missionary; these classes are often not only the most neglected, but also the most influential, namely the government and professional classes. Rarely identified with the "foreign missionaries," the "nonprofessional" often moves in circles outside the reach of the church. Openly exposed to the cross-currents of society, he will frequently be more sensitive to political, cultural, and economic trends than some missionaries who are "buried in the bush" or "embedded in a mission compound."

Then, too, in some countries that are hostile to the gospel, refusing to admit conventional missionaries, Christian teachers and engineers are welcome. In other countries from which Christian missions have been ex-

---

3. *Occasional Bulletin from the Missionary Research Library*, November, 1960.

pelled, "nonprofessional" missionaries have been permitted to remain. In most countries today there is a desire for technological advance. Typical of many similar cases is that of a staff member of a university in a major Latin American city, a man who holds a Ph.D. in physics. He is treated with respect, and his personal testimony for Jesus Christ the more heeded, because it is given by a man who is respected for academic ability.

Some "nonprofessional" missionaries receive ample remuneration, sacrificially using their income to begin work for Christ that is crying to be done, but which the conventional missionary has neither the money nor time to begin.

In many countries the professional missionary has been delighted with the help given by his "nonprofessional" brothers in Christ, be it the service of a mining engineer who used his knowledge to install electric wiring in a mission hospital, the assistance of servicemen's wives who have volunteered to use their nursing skills in missionary clinics, or the advice of professional men in close contact with officials in government circles.

In every country the citizen of tomorrow is influenced by the teaching of today. Vocational missionaries serving in all levels of education have aided the missionary enterprise immeasurably by their service in the schoolroom. The pity is that there are not more of them. There is probably no more effective "nonprofessional" missionary work than that in education in all of its branches.

168

Disadvantages

All this is part of the positive side of a nonprofessional ministry. There is a negative side, too. Many who have traveled abroad in various capacities as "nonprofessional" missionaries have discovered, sometimes with a jolt, that their status carries very real limitations as well as opportunities. Perhaps the greatest frustration is in the matter of language and communication. The missionary who travels abroad with a mission board will normally discover that, for the first years of his service, he is not expected to do anything but concentrate on the language or languages of his new country. The "nonprofessional" missionary usually has no such opportunity, and unless he has an unusual flair for the language, or lives in a country where his native tongue is used, he is likely to find the language barrier an almost insuperable one.

Many have traveled abroad, thrilled with the knowledge that their qualifications as a teacher or engineer have made it possible for them to enter a country that refuses to allow Christian missionaries within its borders, only to find that the local government will not allow them to "proselytize." Thus they are forbidden to speak to its citizens about the One whom they have come to serve. Moreover, since the company or agency that sends them is most anxious to spare any offense to the national government, it is often punctilious in enforcing the "nonproselytizing" clause.

Then there are limitations of time and energy which

169

easily become a ready source of frustration. The primary responsibility of the "nonprofessional" missionary will be to perform his daily duties in a manner that will glorify the Lord. Many times he may well discover that when he has done this, there is little time or energy remaining for "extracurricular" activities.

Another liability is the fact that the continuity of "nonprofessional" missionary work may be seriously jeopardized by secular transfers which create unforeseen vacuums for which there are no replacements.

In some ways, perhaps the most serious danger facing the "nonprofessional" missionary is that of becoming spiritually disoriented. Because he is not in need of financial support from home, he rarely enjoys the intimate prayer support of Christians in a home church in the way that a professional missionary does. Moreover, he is not subject to the discipline which stems from either mission board or local church. In such a situation, if the missionary deviates from his original purpose, no machinery exists to control or withdraw him, and he can become a serious embarrassment to the mission of the church.

In this hour of history it is imperative that the total resources of the Church of Christ be mobilized in the task of evangelizing the world. In this God-given task the role of the "nonprofessional" missionary is likely to become more and more indispensable, especially in the field of education.

One important question a potential "nonprofessional"

missionary must ask himself and answer with brutal honesty is: "Has my witness to Jesus Christ in the homeland been such that I am encouraged to think that it will influence the lives of people abroad?" To send abroad people who are simply likeable and sincere, yet as Christians spiritually ineffective—this will do little to advance the cause of Jesus Christ, however many may go, and however well-equipped professionally they may be.

It is imperative that the "nonprofessional" should guard against the danger of spiritual disorientation. He may safeguard against such a possibility by seeking active fellowship with a local church or individual missionaries, thus tacitly recognizing the value of mutual correction and encouragement among believers. For some this has meant being an associate member of a mission board, although others feel that their freedom would be compromised by such an arrangement. It goes without saying that such individuals must have learned to draw continual supplies of grace from God by intimate and disciplined devotional habits, and through these to maintain spiritual depth and vitality.

A dual mission membership may prove to be the only realistic answer to this problem in many needy areas in the world today. Some advantages of such an arrangement which should be considered include the following:

1. Mission orientation could be extended to "nonprofessionals," in the homelands, so that the long ex-

perience of the past might be shared beneficially. This would make possible close cooperation between professionals and "nonprofessionals" on the field.

2. Field orientation could be extended to "nonprofessionals" in such areas as language, cultural anthropology, and ethnic religion. They would thereby be more likely to appreciate the country in which they have chosen to live and serve.

3. Church orientation could be extended to "nonprofessionals" by national pastors as well as field mission leaders. This would make possible the best type of natural identification with the life and witness of the national church, as well as participation in it.

4. Patterns of mutual consultation, spiritual fellowship, order and discipline could be established. This would result in fewer personal failures, and more oneness and continuity in the over-all task of accomplishing the missionary purpose of God for each country.

5. Making available to "nonprofessionals" the facilities of schools for children, medical services, homeland hostels for teenagers, and vacation and furlough accommodations, might contribute to making possible longer over-all field services for "nonprofessionals."

6. Since the Church in the homelands is primarily involved in overseas service by its provision of personnel, prayer, and financial support to its mission societies, this dual membership would mean that the lives and witness of "nonprofessionals" overseas would come within the sphere of its concern. "Nonprofessionals"

would thereby gain a greater sense of the scriptural and strategic relevance of their work overseas.

7. Should political conditions demand that professional missionaries leave early, there would be no need for a violent rupture of their activities in that part of the world. "Nonprofessionals," fully integrated in a national church that had already become accustomed to their presence and contribution, would continue the ministry. Actually, before the final crisis arose, imaginative mission leadership might even maneuver selected professionals into the "nonprofessional" category and thus anticipate the approaching adjustment.

The difficulties, however, should not be underestimated, and every situation would have to be considered on its individual merits, taking into account the local politico-cultural situation as well as the actual or implied policy of the secular corporation or employer.

More and more openings are presenting themselves for this type of missionary service, and it is to be hoped that we shall see an increasing number of men and women, called by Jesus Christ and empowered by the Holy Spirit, making their impact upon every stratum of society in countries throughout the world. Such a lay ministry is desperately needed and long overdue. Because of the nature of the struggle today, the Church may need increasingly her guerrilla forces.

173

174

Chapter 9: **Facing the Cities**

O NE NOTABLE CHANGE in the social pattern of the last hundred and fifty years has been the drift of population from the country to the town and the subsequent growth of big cities. In 1800, 2.4 per cent of the world population lived in cities of 20,000 inhabitants or more. By 1950, the percentage had risen to 20.9. In actual figures, the number of people living in such cities in 1800 was 21.7 million; in 1950 it was 502.2 million. In the first fifty years of this century the trend to the cities has accelerated. Between 1800 and 1850 the increase in the percentage of the world's population living in cities was slight—from 2.4 per cent to 4.3 per cent. But in the same length of time from 1900 to 1950, the increase jumped from 9.2 per cent to 20.9 per cent.[1] And in Latin America the proportion of the total popu-

---

1. United Nations Secretariat, Bureau of Social Affairs, *Report on the World Social Situation* (New York: United Nations, 1957), p. 114.

lation living in cities in 1955 was almost as high as 44 per cent.[2]

This trend is reflected in the growth of the "millionaire cities" (cities with a population of one million or more). In 1900 there were only eleven millionaire cities in the world. In 1925 there were 56, and by 1955 there were 83. One particularly significant aspect of this trend is the growth of cities in underdeveloped areas. In 1935, Europe had twice as many millionaire cities as Asia; now Asia has more than Europe.[3] In 1900, the number of Asians living in cities of one hundred thousand or more totaled 19.4 million. By 1950 there were 105.6 million—a gain of 444 per cent![4] Jakarta is an ideal illustration of this rapid growth. Its population was 500,000 in 1930, but by 1955 it had risen to nearly three million![5] Perhaps the most surprising fact of all is that the largest proportion of city dwellers in the world (in cities of 20,000 and over) is found in Asia—33.8 per cent as compared with Europe's 27.5 per cent and North America's 13.9 per cent.[6]

Reasons for Urbanization

A number of factors have combined to make possible the growth of city life. Prior to the twentieth century,

2. *9th Mission Executives Retreat, Winona Lake, Indiana, 1960 Report* (Evangelical Foreign Mission Association), p. 7.
3. Audrey M. Lambert, "Millionaire Cities," *Economic Geography*, XXXII, No. 4 (October, 1956).
4. United Nations, *Report*, p. 114.
5. Lambert, *op. cit.*
6. United Nations, *Report*, p. 115.

overcrowding and the contamination of food and water supplies caused health conditions in the cities to be worse than in rural areas. Today, however, modern medical science has reduced the infant mortality rate in the cities to a figure considerably below that in the rural areas.

Number of Deaths per 1,000 Live Births[7]

Argentina	68.2	Buenos Aires	37
Brazil	150	Rio de Janeiro	109
Japan	60.1	Tokyo	42
United States	29.2	New York	25
England & Wales	29.9	London	26

Improved methods of transportation have ensured the provision of adequate food and necessities for a large concentration of people—no small task—while the effects of local and periodic famines have been alleviated. A strike of transportation workers in any big city in the U.S. quickly reminds us of the importance of transportation; it is a veritable lifeline for any large city.

In many parts of the world, the standard of living in the rural areas is pathetically low. The plight of the Indians in the Andes Mountains in Peru and Bolivia, for example, is unforgettable. In Peru, the per capita income of the whole country is $50 per year, whereas in Lima it is $250. It is not difficult to see why people move to the cities. Then, too, it is often extremely dan-

7. *Ibid.*, p. 123.

gerous to live in the country, particularly where war, brigandage, and unsettled political conditions are rife. As a result many have sought for the comparative shelter of the city. The phenomenal growth of the city of Jakarta was due in large measure to the unsettled and precarious conditions throughout Java.

Probably the greatest single desire of many people in underdeveloped countries is for education, a desire that amounts to a craving on the part of many. The city usually offers superior opportunities for education for parents and children alike. Also, the achievement of independence by many countries in Asia and Africa and the highly centralized nature of modern government tend to the concentration of people in a few state and provincial capitals.

But the greatest single factor in the development of city life is industrialization. The growth of modern industry has called for great supplies of labor. The hope of a brighter future and, in some parts of Africa, the efforts of industrial recruiters have done much to lure thousands from rural areas to settle in the cities.

The Impact and Importance of Cities

The city is invariably the center of government, both national and provincial, and its influence is felt in every corner of the country and by all classes of people.

Cities are usually, also, the centers of education, resulting in a great concentration of college and university students in a comparatively small area. No class in

177

the world is more influential—both actually and potentially—than the student and professional class, which is one of the reasons why the Communist Party is so active in cities throughout the world.

The city dwellers who come from the country are generally the younger, more ambitious and vigorous men and women, who are galled with the poverty around them. They come to the cities to find advancement. Frequently opportunists, sometimes dishonest, they are usually the energetic and progressive individuals.

A disruptive influence

Even though the younger, more aggressive element of the rural population tends to migrate to the city, this does not mean that the whole of a city's population is culturally above average. The steady flow of unskilled labor from the country to the city becomes a glut on the labor market, and many individuals are unable to find good or steady employment. Thus are formed the vast, appalling slums that characterize so many of the large cities in Africa, Asia, and Latin America.

Then, too, the gulf that exists between modern city life and the traditional life of the village is sometimes the equivalent of hundreds or even thousands of years of civilization and development.[8] The man from the country arriving in the city is faced with a world at once stimulating and baffling. Familiar landmarks are

8. *Ibid.*, p. 112.

missing. Tribal values have become nonexistent, while morals lapse in the anonymity of city life. Great changes are demanded in the pattern of living, and it is hard to know how much of the old should be retained, how much rejected or suspended. To this dilemma must be added a sense of insecurity and the gnawing pangs of loneliness. For those who seek an easy escape from reality, there is the palliative of the bar and the prostitute.

Even if a whole family should move to the city, it still is not free from the problems inherent in the migration. Such migration often means (1) a shift from the family unit of labor to paid employment of individuals; (2) paid employment, in turn, leads to great equality of family members and can undermine parental authority; (3) which frequently causes members of the family to leave home in order to find employment. Under the pressure of such adverse circumstances, the family, formerly the basic unit of society, disintegrates with alarming rapidity.

Spiritual significance

It is clear from the Scripture and from history that cities have always had a strategic significance in the purposes of God. This can be seen in the Old Testament from the role of Jerusalem, and from the ministry of many of the prophets.

In the New Testament the Church was born and nurtured in a city (Jerusalem), even though the apostles were mostly country men. When the center of missionary activity shifted from Jerusalem, it was transferred to Antioch, which became another strategic city in God's redemptive purpose.

Cities played a particularly important part in the missionary ministry of the Apostle Paul, and received almost all of his attention. The significance of this principle has been clearly stated by the Rev. Robert C. D. Brow, of the Bible and Medical Missionary Fellowship in Allahabad, India, in a lecture given at the London Bible College in December, 1958, from which we quote at some length:

> In approaching this discrepancy between the New Testament standards and the Church's achievement, we must first make sure that our definition of "fully evangelized" is the same as Paul's. It certainly could not mean that Paul himself, or even his personal assistants, had spoken to every person in the area. It would have been impossible to do this in even one of the provincial capitals where Paul spent most of his time, and there is no evidence that he ever evangelized village areas. The smallest towns in which he worked were those of Galatia, and even these were trade centers big enough to have a Jewish synagogue. How then could Paul claim that the whole area was fully evangelized? As Roland Allen made clear in his book *Missionary Methods: St. Paul's or Ours?* Paul contented himself with planting a church in each center of trade and communications, and through these churches the whole surrounding area heard about and had access to the Christian gospel. A text which perfectly expresses

this method is I Thessalonians 1:8, where Paul writes to the church established in the administrative center of the whole province of Macedonia. "From you sounded out the word of the Lord not only in Macedonia and Achaia, but also in every place your faith to God-ward is spread abroad; so that we need not to speak any thing." Notice the significant words, "so that we (the missionaries) need not to speak any thing."

. . . .

We have already seen that we cannot visualize Paul selecting a village area, where no-one else was working, building a mission station, seeking out Gentiles one by one, and gathering the converts on his mission compound. In the Mediterranean he operated from Antioch, the third city of the Roman Empire, he spent about three years in Corinth, which was one of the largest commercial centers of the empire, and his other long stay was in Ephesus, the capital of the province of Asia and the center of trade for Asia Minor.[9]

As Christians we certainly have no reason to deplore the growth of cities throughout the world. On reflection, they present us with an unsurpassed opportunity. The concentration of large numbers of people provides the ideal field for widespread evangelism, since by means of vigorous indigenous churches established in strategic centers, whole areas and even countries can be reached with the gospel.

---

9. Robert C. D. Brow, "Paul's Missionary Methods and the New India," *The Christian Graduate*, XII (December, 1959), 144, 145. Reprinted as "How Paul Would Evangelize India" in *His*, XXI (February, 1961), 12–16, 26.

As communication centers, cities offer unrivalled facilities, human and technological, for the rapid spread of the gospel. As administrative centers, they offer possibilities of influencing all classes with the gospel, including students. The very disrupting forces implicit in societal change can make a man more receptive to a gospel and a way of life that are new to him.

The Challenge to the Church

The city offers unforeseen opportunities to the Church. Simultaneously, it constitutes a formidable challenge—a challenge which remains to be met.

The Cotton Textile Mills Association in Bombay, in careful sociological studies made over the years, discovered Christians among their employees; yet the Christian church had lost them when they moved from the country to the city. One missionary society claims that it lost over 10,000 rural Christians as they moved into the city of Calcutta.[10]

To quote from Robert Brow again:

Now it is true that during the nineteenth century the great cities in India were the first to be occupied. Starting from Calcutta, Carey planned a string of mission stations in key cities on the Ganges, which was then the main artery of communications. Centers like Bombay, Delhi and Lucknow were among the first to be chosen as strategic locations by the early missionary

10. Henry P. Jones, "Urban and Industrial Missions," *Occasional Bulletin from the Missionary Research Library*, X, No. 5 (June 15, 1959).

societies. Succeeding waves of missionaries, however, especially those from newer evangelical missionary societies, tended to deploy further and further into remote areas. In North India today, as in many other mission areas, Evangelicals now have very little influence in the key cities, and our whole missionary program has been weakened in consequence. It is possible that the lack of response in village areas is caused by the lack of evangelical churches in the cities. Although the big cities of North India have numerous large churches with impressive buildings, few of these would have a prayer meeting, Bible class, or the kind of virile missionary interest described in the church at Antioch (Acts 11:20–30, Acts 13:1–3 and Acts 14:26–28).[11]

The failure of the Church, then, is basically three-fold. First, she has failed to keep those members who have migrated from the country to the city. Secondly, she has failed to make an impression on the city masses with the gospel. Thirdly, she has failed to produce the kind of city church with a missionary heart that reaches out to evangelize the surrounding rural area.

It is to the credit of the Church that she has continually sought to cross new frontiers and to assail fresh barriers. Her penetration of jungles and tribes, the crossing of deserts and mountains, the reduction of hundreds of languages into writing, all have been commendable and even heroic. But the failure to reach the cities has been, up to this point, tragic; if it continues,

---

11. Brow, *op. cit.*, p. 145.

it will be disastrous and inexcusable. The failure has been as equally marked in the Western world as in the underdeveloped countries. It is as true of London and New York as of Calcutta and Buenos Aires.

In such circumstances the Church is not wholly unmindful of her responsibility. Almost every branch of Christendom has been exercised by the problem. Many conferences have been held, reports written, and programs organized.

Lessons to Be Learned

One notable exception to this failure of the Church has been the Pentecostal group. In many countries their success has been phenomenal, as is evident in several Latin America cities, notably in Chile and El Salvador. The following statistics for the Assemblies of God in the city of San Salvador are of great interest. For fourteen years this group had one small church in one of the poorer sections of the city. After a fifteen-week open air evangelistic campaign, there followed a period of remarkable growth that continues to this day.

	Churches	Church Members	Sunday School Attendance	Sunday School Classes	Branch Sunday Schools
1956	1	16	100	8	none
1960	20	1,200	7,700	260	155

Today there are 175 Sunday schools in all parts of this city of 300,000, and they have 2½ per cent of the population (one in every forty) studying the Word of Life.

Thousands more are being contacted by the daily radio broadcasts and weekly telecasts.[12]

As in any human work, there are weaknesses. It is true that the ministry of the Assemblies of God has been very largely limited to the very poor classes. But whether or not we agree with our Pentecostal friends on every detail, we have much to learn from them. What are some of the contributing factors to their effectiveness? The answers to such a question could well teach us an object lesson. Among the outstanding features of this work of God are:

1. *An emphasis upon the person and work of the Holy Spirit*. In a day when the Church has come to expect very little in terms of the supernatural, the Pentecostal groups characteristically expect the Holy Spirit to do the unusual thing, and they do not limit themselves to human resources. In talking with the missionaries in El Salvador, one finds that again and again they come back to the centrality of the person and work of the Holy Spirit in their teaching and in their ministry.

2. *Rigid implementation of indigenous church principles*. The entire work of the Assemblies of God in the country of El Salvador, including radio programs, telecasts, Bible institute and literature work, has been done by a total missionary staff of six missionary families and one single woman.

---

12. A personal letter from the Rev. Arthur Lindvall, Assemblies of God missionary in San Salvador, November, 1960.

Although the Assemblies of God have been working in the country of El Salvador for thirty years, it is only in the last seven or eight years that the work has expanded rapidly. This expansion seems to have coincided with a period of rigid implementation of the indigenous method as described in the book *On the Mission Field, The Indigenous Church*, by Melvin L. Hodges. Mr. Hodges is the Secretary for Latin America for the Assemblies of God.

3. *The mobilization of every Christian in the work of evangelism.* Every Christian is encouraged to participate in one way or another, and he feels not only that he belongs to the group, but that he is needed by the group. As soon as a person becomes a Christian, he is expected to begin witnessing, and soon after to start a Sunday school class in his own home. This method encourages the fullest utilization of every member of the church.

In the work of the Assemblies of God, the greatest importance is placed upon the lay preachers. Each lay preacher is authorized by a local presbyter who is a superintendent minister of about four or five churches. The authorization is signed by the district presbyter and pastor, and a secretary of the local church. This is not based upon any course of completed instruction, but upon an evident love for the Lord and some spiritual gift. This authorization lasts for six months, and if the lay preacher keeps busy and active for the Lord, it is renewed. If he does not, then it lapses. This has the twofold effect of giving the man status and authority and at the same time keeping a measure of control over his ministry.

4. *Simplicity in method.* Worshipping often in private homes, most of the churches remain very small. This keeps expenses to a minimum and provides both tasks and responsibility for everybody. Each church is encouraged to open as many preaching points as possible and to foster officially recognized lay pastors. Each church becomes the progenitor of further out-stations. Thus the principle of "multiply and divide" has become a significant factor in the growth of the work.

Meeting the Challenge

As we consider the whole matter of urbanization and the opportunities and problems that it presents to the Church, certain factors need to be borne in mind while lessons need to be learned and applied from the successes and failures of the past.

1. The rediscovery of the laity

A significant milestone in a return to New Testament church doctrine is the rediscovery of the meaning of "laity" or "laos" as the whole people of God, the entire congregation. Throughout the world in almost every community there is a growing emphasis upon the importance and ministry of the rank and file Christian. Elsewhere in this book we have pointed out that if the Church is to survive the challenge of communism, there must be a much greater emphasis upon the practical outworking of the priesthood of all believers. What is vital for us to recognize is that this is demanded by the New Testament as well as by circumstances. It is not merely an expedient; it is a principle.

A bane of the Church in the twentieth century is professionalism. The more complex our society and the more ecclesiastical our method, the greater this threat becomes. It should be noted that the first geographic expansion of the Church is recorded in Acts 8:1, and when this took place the *apostles were left behind in Jerusalem*. They had an important part to play and they took part in the consolidation of the work, but it pleased God then to use the "rank and file" in the expansion of the Church, and He has done so many times since.

Historically, when God has moved in revival He has worked through every member of the body of Christ, and in most cases the impetus for such revival has been maintained by the ministry of groups of unordained preachers, some of whom were quite unsophisticated but possessed natural talent and spiritual gifts, were steeped in the Word of God and, above all, had a deep experience of the power of God in their own lives.

It is unfortunate that in recent years it has been left to a small segment of the Church, and also a number of cults, to demonstrate the necessity of calling upon every believer to play his part in the maintenance and expansion of the Church. There is a tragic side to this failure. Not only does it contribute to a failure to evangelize, leaving the average Christian languishing for want of work, but it ignores the intended ministry of the Holy Spirit who indwells *every* believer.

The cities can best be reached, not by a flood of foreign missionaries (a dim prospect anyhow) but by a missionary-minded, trained, and oriented native church, encouraged in its early stages by a missionary or national who is wholly bent on transmitting his vision of an expanding native church.

2. The selection and training of ministers

One of the encouraging developments of recent years has been the recognition that ministerial training must be practical as well as academic. Some seminaries are thus encouraging their students to take a year out before their final year and to spend it in some kind of practical ministry; others are developing a program whereby the student will pursue some practical ministry while continuing his studies. Such an approach constitutes a notable advance in ministerial training.

It is worth considering the policy of Charles Haddon Spurgeon, who was not only a wonderfully effective preacher but also a great trainer of men. In the introduction to a book of lectures that he delivered to ministerial students at his "Pastor's College," he writes:

The institution [the Pastor's College] receives no man in order to make him a preacher, but it is established to help in the further education of brethren who have been preaching with some measure of success for two

189

> years at the least. . . . Men in whom piety, zeal and
> the indwelling Spirit are to be found need not fear re-
> fusal at our doors. . . .[13]

Spurgeon was a great believer in an educated ministry. But his whole approach was based on the principle
that only God was able to make a minister, and that the
most a ministerial training institution could do was to
take a God-given gift and develop its effectiveness. It
is not merely a matter of giving a seminary student some
experience (as with a medical doctor and his intern-
ship), but a recognition that although we may be able
to produce a medical doctor by subjecting him to a
course of study and practical experience, we cannot so
produce effective ministers and missionaries. In fact,
we cannot produce them at all; only God can.

With our highly developed and protracted system
of education, it may not be possible to institute Spurgeon's rule—two years of proven, effective Christian
service before acceptance for ministerial training. But
more could be done along this line, both in screening
candidates for missionary service and in preparation of
indigenous leadership on the mission field.

One of the best demonstrations of the value of practical training for pastors is seen, at a simple level, among
the Assemblies of God. Following a period as a licensed
lay preacher, a man is authorized to be "an exhorter."
After he has worked as an exhorter satisfactorily for
two years, he becomes a licensed preacher. Finally, af-

---

13. *Lectures to My Students*, First Series (London: Marshall, Mor-
gan & Scott, Ltd., n.d.), pp. vii–viii.

ter five years of satisfactory preaching service and the completion of the whole course of the Bible school, a man is ordained as a pastor. The Bible school course consists of four months of study, followed by months of work in the field; the training period consists of four four-month terms spread over a four-year period.

The whole training is obviously of a very practical and elementary nature, but the missionaries insist that this is inevitable owing to the educational limitations of their pastors. It should be noted that a man is ordained less on the basis of the studies he has completed than on the work he has done. This is a marked contrast to the general policy of the Church of Jesus Christ today.

Furthermore, for the individual Christian, few principles are more important to grasp right now, at whatever stage we may be in Christian growth or in academic preparation. As Christians, we are indwelt by the Holy Spirit and are encouraged to "earnestly desire the higher gifts" (I Corinthians 12:31). Let us earnestly seek God for the spiritual effectiveness that can come only from Him.

3. The allocation of means

In view of the strategic priority of the cities, we must speedily allocate generous resources in order to reach them. This task will require carefully selected and trained personnel. It will also demand money. It is hard to resist the suspicion that one of the attractions of rural missionary work is that it is generally considerably

191

less expensive. The cost of living in some cities, in Latin America and elsewhere, is almost unbelievably high; higher even than in New York or Chicago. One missionary from India has stated frankly, "My mission cannot afford to work in the cities, . . . it costs too much," and he himself pointed out how ironical it is that the mission of which he is a member prides itself on its insistence that God is well able to meet all needs of its workers.

If we are to evangelize our generation, we must recognize that well over one-fifth of this generation is living in cities, that the strategic importance of that segment of the population is great, and that the New Testament gives us a clear indication of the importance of reaching these city dwellers with the gospel.

Of all the areas of service open to the Church, few present such an opportunity or such a challenge as the growing cities of the world. By allocating key personnel to this strategic ministry; by assiduous training of national leaders for this work; by a heavy concentration of prayer and effort upon developing virile, reproducing churches in the cities of the world; by the harnessing of every Christian in the task of evangelism; by the allocation of funds, and above all, by praying for an outpouring of the Holy Spirit in a movement of revival, we must work toward a significant spiritual breakthrough in the cities. This should be our immediate goal for the so-called "homeland" as well as for the overseas mission fields.

Chapter 10: **Reaching the Strategic: Students**

A NEW VOICE is making itself heard around the world. A voice of youth and of vigor. It is the voice of the student.

There is nothing new about student demonstrations. Traditionally, students have been expected to let off steam, to hold parades and demonstrations, and their antics have been regarded with tolerant amusement on the part of the older and more staid segments of society. The voice of the students, however, cannot be dismissed so lightly in this generation.

When President Eisenhower planned a visit to Tokyo, it was the Japanese students who thwarted his plans. When the government of Syngman Rhee in Korea was discredited, it was the students who toppled him from power. When Vice President Nixon was stoned in Venezuela, it was the students who did it. No longer is it true to say only that students are the leaders of tomorrow. In many countries of the world, they are the leaders of today.

A growing class

Perhaps the most remarkable development in education during the past decade or so has been less the spectacular advance in various fields of study than the great expansion that has taken place in the availability of learning for the masses.

For centuries education has been the privilege of a few and its aim the creation of an educated elite. Today, such a philosophy has become outmoded. The availability of education is seen in the rising number of college students throughout the world. In Great Britain in the year 1958–59, there were 100 per cent more students studying in universities than prior to 1939. "Up till 1939 only 1 in 60 of any age-group reached a university. Now the figure is about 1 in 30."[1] Also, significantly, three-fourths of the full-time university students in the United Kingdom are aided by scholarships or other awards, of which large numbers are granted by the state or by local educational authorities.

In the U.S.A. 40 per cent of all young people of college age are enrolled in colleges, universities, schools of nursing, or technical institutions, and the enrollment

---

1. Sir James Duff, *Universities in Britain* (London: Longmans, Green & Co. Ltd., 1959), p. 13. Note: It is impossible to compare these figures accurately with those for the U.S.A., as much of what ranks as university study in the U.S.A. takes place in Britain in technical colleges.

of three and a half million in 1960 is expected to become six million by 1970.

While this is, of course, a far higher proportion than in the rest of the world, education is so obviously the key to individual progress and to national prosperity that, throughout the world, there are few sacrifices that young people are not willing to make to obtain a college degree. In some countries students accept a near starvation level of diet in order to finance a college career.

A strategic class

That this class is strategic politically should be obvious to all. These are the people who in coming years will dominate the leadership of countless national and local governments, and through teaching posts, will mold the minds and lives of countless citizens of the world. Taking their place of leadership in the legal, medical, and teaching professions, the fields of scientific and industrial research, government, finance, business, labor, and industry, they will exercise a decisive influence on their countries, and sometimes alter the course of events far beyond the boundaries of their own countries.

That they are politically strategic is confirmed by the attention given students by the communist states. On May 26, 1961, *Time* magazine reported that Communist China was suffering from such an acute shortage of paper that some newspapers in that country had reduced their pages to half the usual number, and that the 150 periodicals on sale in 1959 had dwindled to a dozen. But, *Time* added significantly, "The only exception to the paper austerity program are exports. By Mao's order, the gospel according to Peking is still flowing as freely as ever to the uncommitted countries of Latin America and Africa." It has been reported that China is spending one-half million dollars a year in postage alone in shipping propaganda to Latin America —and much of this is destined for students. No class is wooed more assiduously by the Communists than the students of the world, and they have been all too successful in their advances. Sensitive as they are to political issues, often idealistic, and acutely aware of the injustices of the countries in which they live, students provide a fertile breeding ground for Marxism.

But if they are strategic politically, we must grasp the fact that they are just as strategic spiritually. In this day of dramatic developments in the affairs of men and nations, we dare not overlook the fact that in any country from which missionaries may be compelled to evacuate, the existence of a hard core or cadre of disciplined and dedicated Christians in the professional classes will be a necessity if a truly vigorous national church is to survive.

There are those who regard an approach to the educated classes as out of step with the gracious call of God in the gospel. Abraham Lincoln remarked that God obviously loved common people because He made so many of them. And there are those who would quote the following passage in support of this thesis:

> For consider your call, brethren; not many of you were wise according to worldly standards, not many were powerful, not many were of noble birth; but God chose what is foolish in the world to shame the wise . . . (I Corinthians 1:26, 27).

But we must guard against assuming that God puts a priority on ignorance and the inability to secure higher education. The fact remains, an academic education is becoming increasingly the norm in society. With everyone striving for education, the Church dare not assume a posture of indifference or withdrawal. Then too, the history of the Church is replete with the evidence of God's bringing men of great gifts and academic training to himself and using them in a significant way to advance His cause. He chose a Paul, an Augustine, a Luther, a Calvin, a Wesley, and a Whitefield to change significantly the course of events in their own countries, and to extend the blessing of His salvation to untold millions.

A needy class

Until the age of eighteen, the student has lived in the threefold structure of home, school, and often church, synagogue, temple, or mosque. Usually, there are customs, rules, and regulations in the home with its traditions. In school the courses are pretty well laid

197

out, though with some degree of freedom in later schooling. For many students there is some sort of religious training in the family tradition. Now the student, particularly if he goes away from home to study, leaves this threefold structure. He comes into the exciting new atmosphere of the modern university. For him it is a time of testing, questioning, and doubting. In itself this is good. Plato said, "The unexamined life is not worth living." Someone has said, "If a man is not a revolutionary at the age of twenty, he has no heart; if he is still a revolutionary at the age of thirty he has no head." While overstated, this illustrates college years. They are turbulent and exciting. There is the search for truth and the adventure of the mind, at least where education has not been reduced to the trade-school level, as in some U.S. colleges. All this seems to be universally characteristic of the university student.

For instance, Islam is considered to be the most inflexible of religions and to command a fanatical loyalty and devotion on the part of its followers. But the leaders of Islam are concerned because many of their young people in their universities have been pried loose from the beliefs and customs of their fathers; while remaining Muslims culturally, they have lost faith in their religion and are living in a spiritual vacuum.

Much the same is true in Latin America. Generally speaking, the students have little faith in Roman Catholicism, feeling that it may be acceptable "for women and children," but that it is not relevant to the contemporary situation and can offer no satisfying answer to the great problems of life.

"What am I here for?" "What is the purpose of life?" "Is there anything worth devoting my life to?" These are the questions that one hears continually on campuses throughout the world. A student leader of a national denominational movement declared that he was not a Christian and was not convinced of the existence of God. On being asked whether he did not feel it to be inconsistent for him to lead a Christian movement and hold such views, he answered that he saw no contradiction as long as he was "seeking for the truth." His honesty as an individual is probably to be commended, but his views are hardly to be tolerated in a position of Christian responsibility.

In many parts of the Orient students have become cynical concerning their ancestral religion and many do not even profess to be nominal followers of any religion at all. This characteristic of the student world need not surprise us. When the student enters the university, he is usually urged to take nothing for granted and to learn to question everything, including the beliefs of his parents. In the case of the student from a primitive background, he rapidly sees that many of the supernatural beliefs of his people are untenable in the light of modern science. He is faced with the painful problem of how much of his past to reject; not infrequently he decides to reject almost all of it.

Just as the allied victory in World War II discredited

199

emperor worship in Japan, so other forces have been at work undermining the religion of students in other countries. It is difficult for a Hindu student to accept without reservation the importance of the "sacred cow" after he has become aware of the blight the very same animal places upon the nation's economy.

What is the Tunisian student to do, after being carefully indoctrinated all his early life with the traditional Muslim view that for one month every year no good Muslim will swallow one mouthful of food or drink from sunrise to sunset, when he hears the Muslim president of his country announce that they are engaged in a "holy war against poverty" and should therefore break the Fast of Ramadan? Some students are able to reconcile these conflicts, but others are unable to do so and become disillusioned with their own religion in particular and all religion in general.

Basically, of course, the problem is spiritual rather than intellectual. "For since, in the wisdom of God, the world did not know God through wisdom . . ." (I Corinthians 1:21). There is a vacuum in the heart of man that can never be filled by learning per se, but only by God himself. Although the students' minds are being stimulated, their motivations center more in their hearts than in their heads. The presentation of the gospel to the student must be intelligent, but it is tragic if it is merely intellectual. Many young men and women today are not primarily concerned with ideas, per se,

200

but are seeking for something that can meet their spiritual, intellectual, and emotional needs. When the student seeks for bread, we must be sure that we ourselves are not offering what to him is a stone.

A critical class

The very nature of the students' training and environment makes them dissatisfied with pat answers, with religious jargon, with sectarianism. Five per cent of intellectual inaccuracy is enough to make the student completely dismiss the other 95 per cent of truth that a speaker may present. The presentation of the gospel to the student must be an intelligent one, for the student's heart can rarely receive what his mind rejects.

Students are trained to be suspicious of any authoritarian approach. They expect the gospel to be presented to them in an orderly, reasonable fashion. They expect major premises to be defined and established. For this reason they are inclined to be very critical of an ill-prepared, emotionally presented Christian message. Anyone who has worked with students can testify to the ease with which their attention is gained when they are given messages that are challenging in thought-content, by a speaker who is honest in admitting areas where there is insufficient knowledge to be dogmatic. Students are impressed by the image of a man, his personal appearance, his openness of heart, and his genuine interest in them. They will frankly turn away from

201

the pompous professional religionist who mouths beautiful words, but who does not personally seem to be gripped by them.

A responsive class

It would be absurd to suggest that all students are simply waiting to hear the gospel presented so that they may accept it. In a student congregation, as in any congregation, there will be a few who are openly and avowedly hostile, a large segment that is indifferent, but an important minority who are open and eager to find the truth in Jesus Christ. Typically they do not have as much vested interest in their intellectual and social *status quo* as they will in five or ten years' time, when they are climbing ladders of one kind or another.

It is doubtful whether any type of Christian work is more satisfying than student work. Those students who are really open to spiritual truth display qualities of enthusiasm, receptivity, and dedication that are found in few other classes. Indeed, the reservoir of untapped human resources among the student classes is almost without limitations except for those of our own making.

A neglected class

Ever since the incursions of liberalism at the turn of the century affected the major colleges, universities, and seminaries across the country (leading the evangelicals to establish the Bible school movement),

202

evangelicals have reacted against secular education. Evangelicals have long had a reputation for great missionary fervor and enthusiasm. Such a reputation is probably not undeserved, but it is strange that the same evangelicals have done so little to understand the challenge of the student world and to rise to the challenge and opportunity that it presents. One reason for this undoubtedly is preoccupation with other varied and pressing responsibilities. In this the evangelical is not alone; the entire Protestant community has failed to take the student's doubts and questions seriously.

Elsewhere in this book, mention has been made of the heroic achievements of missionaries in terms of tribal work, rural work, linguistics, etc. But apart from some isolated, exciting examples such as the work of the International Fellowship of Evangelical Students, International Students, Inc., and a meager handful of other agencies, the neglect of the world's students has been so complete as to constitute a rebuke to the Church. In the sight of God, a student is no more important than a peasant or a savage, but at least he is no *less* important.

Jungle work is often more dramatic to present to the public than student work. But a medical doctor, who has worked among a primitive tribe which earlier had murdered the first five missionaries to visit them, and who also has done considerable leprosy work, considers that both these ministries were considerably easier than the student work in which he is now engaged. He regards his present work in the universities as being of first priority in terms of urgency and strategy.

While the Christian public is kept aware of various types of missionary work, portrayed in a stream of superb literature, only occasionally are they given a glimpse of student work. And until recently, few showed much concern for the students of the world. No missionary statesman would wish to withhold recruits and resources from evangelizing the tribes and the rural areas, but neither must he neglect the unique challenge to evangelize students.

Part of the difficulty in student work lies in the fact that evangelicals have tended so to withdraw from the world that they do not understand the world—they feel uncomfortable in the presence of those who belong to it. In North America, sections of the evangelical church have created a distinctive subculture with its own language and thought-forms, its own somewhat sentimental music, and its own criteria of behavior, frequently none of which have any very close relationship to biblical principles. There is in consequence an inability to communicate with those who are outside of "our circle" and who have not been conditioned by similar behavior and speech. After speaking to a group of students in the U.S.A., one minister said, "I was brought up in a Christian home, went to Christian schools, college and seminary, and frankly I cannot communicate with these students. We speak a different

204

language." This is not mainly a matter of education, for many have had a similarly sheltered educational background but have good rapport with twentieth-century students, and many who have not had this particular form of background seem to have succumbed to the same "monastic" tendencies.

A sad part of this trend is that it has robbed us of effectiveness among students in North America. An even sadder thing is that we have exported this same culture, with its characteristic weaknesses and divisive tendencies, in the name of evangelical Christianity to the mission fields of the world. It is now possible to visit almost any other country and hear in their churches the same inferior hymn tunes, the same "special music," even the same intonation on the part of song leaders with the same gestures that one finds at home. All that is changed is the language and perhaps the color of the skin.

It must be said that there are some notable exceptions to this failure to establish rapport with the secular student class in North America. Around the continent there are a handful of churches which are communicating the gospel to students and building them up with great effectiveness. Theirs is an investment which will pay handsome dividends for the universal outreach of the Church.

A group of students in a university in North America recently asked a visiting minister to speak on the subject, "Lost, Lonely, Lustful." When asked why they

205

had chosen this topic, they replied, "These adjectives suggest the three biggest problems confronting students today." This description need not surprise us, for the three problems are as old as man himself—merely, perhaps, accentuated by the atmosphere and emphases of the academic world. The most common characteristic of today's student, especially in the West, seems to be restlessness and purposelessness; he has few and usually transitory goals.

A class to be reached

The size of the vast and growing student class, together with its strategic importance and our past neglect, must lead us to an all-out attempt to reach it by every available means.

One opportunity for reaching the students of the world is right at our front door—an opportunity we dare not miss. There are over 48,000 students from over 140 countries studying in the U.S.A. today, some of whom come from countries closed to Christian missionaries.[2] In October, 1960, there were over 50,000 full-time students from overseas studying in Great Britain.[3]

It is deplorable that many of these students return to positions of leadership in their own countries disillusioned and cynical as a result of their experiences while studying in Western countries. Fortunately, it is also

---

2. *Open Doors 1960* (Institute of International Education, May, 1960), p. 6. 3. *Overseas Students in Britain 1960–1961* (The British Council, October, 1961).

true that an increasing minority have been brought to a personal knowledge of God in Jesus Christ and have returned as ambassadors of Jesus Christ. Thousands of Christians have opened their homes and their hearts to international students, finding not merely satisfying friendships, but from time to time, the encouragement of seeing them enter from darkness into light.[4]

Another means of ministering to students throughout the world, already referred to, is that of teaching overseas. Scattered in universities and technical colleges throughout the world are men and women who have recognized that one of the most effective ways of exposing students in other lands to vital Christianity is to serve abroad as a Christian professor or instructor. There are far more openings than there are people to fill them, and this is certainly something that should be regarded as priority in the thinking and planning of the Church as she faces the future.[5]

Admirable work has also been done by Christians of various nationalities working among the students in many countries of the world. The aim, of course, must be to produce a student work that is indigenous, and the best equipped persons to reach the students of any

4. For Christians particularly interested in learning more about this type of ministry, further information can be obtained by writing to International Student Department, Inter-Varsity Christian Fellowship, 1519 N. Astor, Chicago 10, who publish a booklet, *Guide to International Friendship.*

5. The Inter-Varsity Christian Fellowship is setting up a bureau for vocational witness overseas, and information may be obtained by writing to 1519 N. Astor, Chicago 10, Illinois.

given country are Christian students of that country reaching out to their peers. Those who do such work have great need of spiritual discernment and sensitivity, as they not only evangelize students but train students to reach other students. It would be hard to think of any ministry anywhere that is more important or deserving of prayer and support than the work of those called to minister among overseas students, either in North America or abroad.

It is heartening indeed to see that among many missionary leaders today there is a quickened interest in the whole field of student evangelism and many are seeking for information and ways in which to accomplish this great task. Many mission boards have allocated selected missionary personnel to work with agencies who are engaged full time in universities throughout the world. Still others are encouraging their missionaries to enroll in courses at universities, to become acquainted with students, and to spend part or all of their time in reaching them for Christ. Students from most countries in the world are intensely sensitive to social and political issues, and those who work among them will not gain a responsive hearing for their message unless they, too, are sensitive to issues such as those of social injustice, racial discrimination, and physical hunger.

Although students are sometimes on crowded campuses, they are often lonely. Also, they are usually friendly and informal, and although quick to prick any balloon of pomposity, responsive to friendliness, sincerity, and directness.

We must remember that student groups present us not merely with a challenge to evangelize, but in one sense a partial solution to world evangelization. For, by virtue of their age and education, this group of men and women comprises the greatest reservoir of manpower for the cause of Jesus Christ in the entire world. The strategic possibilities are limitless.

There is no easy way of accomplishing this task, but the need is great, the hour is late, and it is imperative that by our prayers, our support, and the giving of ourselves we seek to reach these countless young men and women with the message of life.

Of all the resources to be mustered in this task, the most pressing need is undoubtedly that of more and more prayer on behalf of this work. The very nature of this type of work means that very frequently the person who is working among students abroad is denied the kind of intimate, close prayer support of a church in the homeland. Surely every church that is really missionary-minded and has a world view will be earnestly considering ways and means to gain the prayer and support of their constituency for this neglected and vital segment of the world that is waiting to be evangelized.

Chapter 11: **Communicating the Message**

THE SCENE was a prison camp. A Red officer disdainfully eyed a captive missionary. "Why," the Communist scoffed, "I can put three pieces of our literature in the hands of any literate Chinese and make a Communist!" This is no idle boast. It could have been made by any number of Communists in any one of many underdeveloped countries. The Communists produce annually at least three pieces of literature for every man, woman, and child on the face of the earth. It has been a significant factor in their conquest of over one-third of the world's total population. And yet according to the French communist newspaper *Peace and Liberty*, "The Gospel is a much more powerful weapon for the renewal of society than is our Marxist philosophy." We might add that the gospel can do much more than renew society. God is desperately anxious to restore and regenerate millions of individual men and women.

210

Literature

Our authority

"The pen is mightier than the sword." Viewed in the light of history, this statement is one we can scarcely doubt to be true. One cannot name a single major revolution or a significant current of events which was not born or stimulated by the printed page. Today as never before we are faced with a battle of ideologies. An atomic stalemate has reduced the sword to a starkly simple instrument of racial suicide. If the pen is mightier today politically, it has always been so, in the long-term view, religiously. Every major religion has its own sacred scriptures or writings and some, such as the Jew, the Muslim, and the Christian, have become known at times as people of the book.

The Christian believes that God has spoken through patriarchs, prophets, priests, kings, apostles—and supremely, through His Son, the Incarnate Word. But if this had not been divinely recorded, then without watering down its original nature as divine revelation it would have become no more than oral tradition (cf. the Talmud). The written Word in combination with the resurrected Christ and the Holy Spirit is the Christian's indispensable basis of authority; and rightly used, his most powerful weapon of offense. Biblical literature thus constitutes the key to effective evangelism— whether in the form of a written exposition (tract or treatise) or simply the Scriptures themselves. Though literature's usefulness in the communication of the gospel was neither fully realized nor utilized until after the advent of the printing press, it is not, like many modern methods, a human device for a divine task. It is as old as the tablets of the law God gave to men at Mount Sinai. It is as ancient and as relevant as the Hebrew Scriptures, the recorded Gospels and the Epistles—in short the whole authoritative canon of Scripture, the Word of God.

The historic testimony

Most of us are well acquainted with the public notice that set in motion a chain of events that split a nation, shook a continent, and shaped the future civilization of the West. It was not, as one might expect, a declaration of war by a powerful secular or ecclesiastical ruler; neither was it the considered opinion of an influential judicial committee or legislative body. It was a theological treatise in Latin by an earnest German monk. The ninety-five theses which Martin Luther nailed to the church door in Wittenberg kindled a flame which still burns wherever Reformation theology prevails. Luther, moreover, followed up his initial protest against the abuses of Rome by a flood of literature in the vernacular German which had a notably wider and more enduring impact than even his fearless and powerful public preaching. More than two hundred years later at a public reading of Luther's Commentary on Romans, John Wesley entered into assurance of salvation. John Calvin's ministry was similarly extended and perpetuated by his skillful use of the printed page.

H. G. Wells, admittedly less notable as an historian than a novelist, but definitely not notable for his sympathy toward Christianity, writes regarding Luther and the Protestant Reformation: "It is not too much to say that paper made that revival of Europe possible."

Tragically, it was not until the end of the eighteenth century that the modern missionary movement began under the originating genius of the shoemaker-scholar William Carey. If the subsequent ministry of literature had been carried on with the same single-hearted devotion and zeal with which the modern missionary pioneers began it, the story of missions might have been different. It was out of Carey's passion to translate the Scriptures that the "Serampore Trio" emerged—that combination of Carey's pen, Ward's printing press, and Marshman's pedagogic skill which laid broad and deep foundations for the coming expansion of the Church. Carey had a controlling hand in the translation of the Bible into more than forty languages.

Again and again, wherever missions made an impact for God, we find the pioneers employing literature. After Carey came men such as Henry Martyn, who in six years produced versions of the Bible in Hindustani, Urdu and Persian; Robert Morrison, the pioneer of Chinese missions, who said that his greatest task was to learn the language and translate the Scriptures; Moffat in South Africa; Williams in the South Pacific; Kalley in South America. Each of their ministries was remarkable for the part literature played. And yet in the years which followed, with certain notable exceptions such as Samuel Zwemer, the Church neglected this God-given instrument. Zwemer, the great apostle to the Muslims, sagely observed, "No other agency can penetrate so deeply, witness so daringly, abide so persistently, and influence so irresistibly as the printed page."

There are many historical instances of the power of literature. When Charles Wesley loaned George Whitefield a book entitled *The Life of God in the Soul of Man* by Henry Scougal, it led to the conversion of that great evangelist to the English-speaking world. Neither must we forget that a simple tract led to the salvation of J. Hudson Taylor, the founder of the China Inland Mission. The pattern is endless.

Today's need for literature

It was still early in the morning, but already the peasants working in the fields had become hot and sticky. The sun was creeping through the shutters of the crumbling adobe buildings. Life was little different for the villagers than it had been for their forebears centuries ago. It was true there had been some changes—a few people were able to read, and there was an unpaved road through the center of the village; but the toil and misery were still with them. The only difference was that they heard regular reports from the outside world of the enormous wealth to be had in the great cities.

Many of the younger people had recently left to make their fortune and further their scanty education.

Slowly the tranquility of the scene was broken by a steadily increasing rumble. Suddenly a heavily laden truck swept round the corner in a cloud of dust. By its sheer speed, it was obviously just passing through on its way to the city. Soon it was gone. But even as the dust settled, bits of paper fluttered to the ground. Like a batch of hawks sweeping in for the kill, the people dropped their bundles and their tasks and scrambled for what, to the outsider observer, might well have been gold nuggets. Little knots of people gathered eagerly round the illustrious few who could read, as stumblingly and excitedly they read the news from the outside world. No, this was certainly not the daily newspaper. It was the good news of an event which took place two thousand years ago—but due to poor communications, the people had not yet fully heard of it. It included an invitation to a free Bible correspondence course. It might easily have been a piece of skillful communist propaganda. Whichever of these two it turned out to be, it would ultimately cause a revolution in the lives of the villagers.

This incident could have happened anywhere in awakening Asia, Africa, or Latin America. It is happening every day. Its significance can be measured by the fact that these people are largely illiterate. As one might expect, the repercussions are infinitely magnified among student readers, while the more-or-less permanent ministry of a magazine or well-stocked bookstore is capable of reaching tens of thousands of city dwellers. Not only is literature an ideal form of reaching individuals, it is the only effective means of meeting the challenge of world population growth.

In previous chapters, we have depicted something of the population explosion and its implications for the Christian mission. In Latin America alone, the population is expected to soar from the present 185,000,000 (less than the population of North America) to a mammoth half billion by the year 2000. After 250 years of the modern missionary movement, no more than 2 per cent of Africa, India, and the Orient are today even nominally Christian. At the same time the literacy rate is climbing even more rapidly. India, for example, with a population in excess of 375,000,000, possesses a 25 per cent literacy rate, whereas it was only 15 per cent several years ago. We must not shrink at the magnitude of the task. God has made provision for this hour. We must act. Already there are encouraging signs of a vast and concerted effort to employ literature on the widely differing fields around the world.

For generations, medicine and education have been the two spearheads of missionary advance. With increasing governmental responsibility in both these spheres, literature is likely to take the lead as the most effective mode of spreading the gospel in many areas. This will not displace medical and educational ministries, but will supplement and solidify them where they already exist, while opening up virgin fields for church-planting operations. It is most significant that literature holds an important key to the establishment of the truly indigenous church. We need look no further than the Apostle Paul for a precedent and an example of how literature stimulated the spiritual vitality of the young churches, without sapping their initiative or their dependence on the Holy Spirit.

There is an urgent need today for good literature to promote the healthy growth of the overseas churches. The abundance of literature available to the English-speaking world is almost an embarrassment when we face up to the paucity of Christian literature available in other languages.

"An African pastor came to a literature conference and said, 'I've walked with God for forty years. My people are filled with questions, and I answer them the best I can, but I can't remember everything. Once in a while I get to bring my questions to the missionary. Each year I get a few of my questions answered, but never all.' Then he pointed at the shelves of English books at the mission station, and said, 'Here you have 300–400 teachers. Whenever you want a question answered, you turn to your books and the answer brings peace to your hearts. You have hundreds of teachers. My people have nothing!' " [1]

---

1. *Conservative Baptist*, October, 1960.

Advantages of literature

One of the must obvious advantages of literature is its ability to be mass-produced once the initial work is completed. No form lends itself more readily to cheap mass-production and distribution than gospel tracts. Concerning the advantages of tracts someone has written the following:

Tracts go everywhere. Tracts know no fear. Tracts never tire. Tracts can be multiplied without end by the press. Tracts can travel at little expense. . . . They can talk to one as well as to the multitude; and to a multitude as well as to one. They require no public room to give their message in; they can tell it in the kitchen or in the store, the parlor or the workshop, in the railway car or in the bus, on the broad highway or in the footpaths through the fields. They take no note of scoffs, or jeers, or taunts. No one can betray them into hasty or random expressions. Though they will not always answer questions, they will tell their story twice, thrice, or four times over if you wish them. And they can be made to speak wisely and well. They can, in short, be made vehicles of all truth; the teachers of all classes; the benefactors of all lands.[2]

There are advantages of literature which are not confined to tracts. It can be said of any form of Christian literature that it can be made to speak clearly, directly, and without the negative impressions created by a foreign accent and foreign face. A faulty grammatical

---

2. Source uncertain.

style can be more easily eliminated on paper than when the missionary himself speaks. And when the national writes literature for his own people, the reader readily detects the authentic flavor of the non-Western writer. Thus besides multiplying his ministry, the national is spared the handicap of a physical or at least mental association with the foreigner. The image of an independent and sympathetic writer with whom the reader may rapidly identify himself—together with his hopes and fears—is a priceless asset with which to commend the message to the reader.

Once written—and written well—literature is free from the downward pull of physical fatigue. It can work twenty-four hours a day, week in and week out, conveying its message without becoming jaded or lukewarm. It requires no vacations, furloughs, or sick leaves. It can be ignored and even mutilated without taking offense, yet when it finally speaks, it often finds the reader alone and open to its message. Sometimes it may become banned by hostile authorities, which makes it more desirable than ever for some. It can be destroyed easily, but makes its reappearance to more sympathetic readers with unabated effectiveness. It proves more patient and persistent than its best authors, while it is notable, above all else, for its constancy. It has never been known to go back on its word. "It always sticks to what it says and never answers back—it is bait left permanently in the pool."

Literature is admirably suited to the present world

situation. Its language can be carefully edited to lessen racial and national elements. It can be screened against "foreignness" and can proclaim its message within the context of the culture it is designed to reach. It can be carefully prepared to accomplish specific tasks. If sufficiently attractive, it can reach even the most prejudiced and proud.

A recent example of the urgent need to increase the use of literature (and one might add, in places crash programs) comes from the Rev. T. E. Lloyd, Home Secretary of the Africa Inland Mission in a statement which he entitled "Lessons from the Congo for Christian Missions":

> Christian literature is today's absolute number one priority in all missionary planning. Without for one moment deprecating the proven value of radio, this can be carried on from outside the country, as is being done today. But while we have opportunity still to work in Africa, it is really urgent that we produce Christian reading matter. It is far harder to send books into countries from outside, especially if their officials introduce regulations and laws to hinder this. Before long it might be impossible to do much about literature for Africa—it is far from impossible now.[3]

Rivals in the field

We would be deluded if we imagined we had the field all to ourselves. Like Paul, writing from Ephesus, we can thank God for an open door, but we must recog-

---

3. In *The Life of Faith*, September 29, 1960.

nize our rivals (I Corinthians 16:9). Communists, Muslims, Roman Catholics, the cults—all are engaged in the battle for the minds of men, and each of them is turning out far more, and often far better, literature than evangelical Christians. It is reported that in India 70 per cent of all available literature comes from communist presses. Even the poorest in India, who are often the most susceptible to communist propaganda, can buy a small library of communist books sufficient to fill a 15-inch shelf—plus a lamp thrown in to read by—for a small amount. *Time* magazine for August 9, 1954, stated: "The press is the greatest of all Communist assets." Meanwhile the Muslims, long noted for their zeal, have recently formed the Koran Society, patterned after the occidental Bible Societies, for the publishing and distribution of the Koran.

The cults, too, have been notoriously successful in propagating their "gospel" by means of literature. The Jehovah's Witnesses produce more than 45 million copies annually of their magazine *Watchtower* in 65 languages; their total production every eight hours would amount to a stack higher than the Empire State Building. For them the results are seen in an annual membership increase of 400 per cent. In Uruguay, South America, 100 Mormon missionaries—almost the equal of the combined total of evangelical workers—swept through the country distributing their literature with great effectiveness. Christian Science, a cult which caters to the intellectual, produces the only

221

daily church newspaper in the world today with a massive worldwide circulation. The same group is causing deep concern among the Jewish rabbis in New York where large numbers of Jewish people are being drawn away from their synagogues.

In a day when tracts and leaflets are recognized as essential to the promotion of almost anything, the evangelical movement around the world produced only slightly more than a billion tracts last year. Our motive is not to match our rivals in quantity produced and distributed, but simply to realize the nature of the struggle in which we are engaged and then, not out of competition but compassion, employ this God-given instrument as effectively and as judiciously as we can. This will not be achieved without a great deal of sacrifice by every Christian, for everyone has a part to play. Only a few will be called to produce literature, but everyone can distribute, and give, and pray. Fortunately there are men and women who have not only a vision of the need for Christian literature but also the God-given ability to meet that need. The *Chicago Daily Tribune* for Thursday, June 22, 1961, carried an article telling of a courageous Conservative Baptist Foreign Missions Society missionary engaged in translating the New Testament into a tribal language in the Congo, who, after evacuating his family, returned to a murderous stretch of country for almost six months to complete the work of translating. He finally left, confident that the native pastors, equipped with the gospel in their own language, will carry on the witness of the Church.

Means and methods

Publishing is a costly and complex undertaking. Because it is not as appealing to the heart and imagination as a personality often is, it is frequently difficult to raise sufficiently large-scale finances for literature. Yet in terms of comparative outreach, literature conserves both funds and personnel. For example, for the same initial investment it takes to set up at least three large self-supporting bookstores in key cities, and employ fifteen or more national Christian workers (paying them good wages), thus providing three large cities with an effective and permanent Christian witness, it would be possible to send only a single young married couple with two children abroad and back for a five year term.[4]

Publishing involves many stages. Original writing and editing, often translation and further editing, production, and marketing—all these take time, money, and trained personnel. The training of nationals to carry on this work in its various stages is the underlying responsibility of all literature workers today. Meanwhile, there is a crying need for almost every type of literature. Bible exposition, theological and doctrinal studies, inspirational and devotional books, biographical and historical works, materials on apologetics, philosophy, and contemporary issues, helps for all aspects of local church life and witness, hymns and spiritual songs, and of course the Scriptures themselves—all

4. David Glass, *Successful Bookstore Management* (Chicago: Moody Literature Mission).

223

are indispensable to the healthy development and corresponding outreach of the Church.

Nowhere is the role of literature more vital and demonstrably effective than in the field of evangelism. As we have already noted, people read everywhere—and everything from tracts to tomes. It seems that the best evangelistic media in the field of literature are magazines, correspondence course invitation tracts, and ad-evangelism—according to the needs of the particular area. In highly literate Japan where the people will read the secular newspapers regularly, ad-evangelism is ideal. In virtually untouched and semi-literate areas such as much of the Middle East, simple correspondence courses have a good deal of appeal in an otherwise hostile environment. Where there is any sort of organized structure in society, Christian magazines have the added advantage of being able to speak to the reader in successive issues. Thus prejudices and misconceptions are broken down gradually. Later, with his sympathy won and his appetite whetted, the reader often becomes a sincere seeker who is able to respond intelligently to either the written or oral gospel.

The value of such Christian magazines as the *Challenges, Lighthouses,* and *Voices* (at least fifteen!) around the world is incalculable. In Africa, one popular Christian magazine stepped up its circulation from scratch to 160,000 in only three years of operation. We need more such magazines with their careful consideration of contemporary social problems as well as their simple but thoughtful presentation of the gospel. As a preliminary to the launching of the larger and costlier magazines, the V.I.P. (vernacular indigenous publication), a much smaller trial or supplementary language edition, has been found an effective tool.

The growth of the correspondence school ministry has been one of the most amazing phenomena in missions in the last decade. All around the globe, correspondence courses are proving their value—with Hindus in India, Buddhists in Thailand, and Muslims in Morocco. Readers in every country are hungrily devouring the Word and answering the simple questions about the passage they have just read. In the Philippines, new enrollments are currently coming in at the rate of more than 1000 a week. The Emmaus Correspondence Courses (Plymouth Brethren) currently offer 35 courses in 60 languages, and to date more than 500,000 have been enrolled. The growth of national correspondence schools in Latin America, the Indian sub-continent, southeast Asia, and to a lesser extent Africa and Europe, is but an indication of the signal contribution these courses are making in ministering to the secret inquirer, the awakened, and the new convert.

By far the most crucial problem facing many literature programs is an efficient distribution and sales program. There are probably more than a dozen proven methods which have been variously adapted to the local situation. However, the two most universal means

225

of distribution are the colporteur and the bookstore. The former is a well-tried method, which not only provides the personal contact but enables even the most illiterate national to play his part in the missionary program. In Vietnam not very long ago, six missionary colporteurs sold more than 2,500 books in two and one-half days in a crowded city. Moreover, the colporteur is often able to combine his selling with house-to-house visitation (see Acts 20:20) with extremely gratifying results in many instances—both in terms of sales and spiritual response.

By contrast the bookstore is a more recent development in the armory of missions. It has proved itself to be not only an excellent distribution center to reach the city throngs (many from out of town) but also a fruitful evangelistic center. Ideally the bookstore should be manned by nationals and should include facilities for reading and counselling. As a sample of its usefulness, a small bookstore in Brazil recorded the sale of 20,000 Bibles, 10,000 New Testaments and 70,000 Scripture portions in one year alone. And other bookstores have even more remarkable sales in the light of the circumstances and the opposition they face.

Programs and problems

The current series of convulsions which ring the globe are unprecedented in human history. While there can be no universal blueprint for an effective literature

226

program, we need to take into account every possible factor which could make or mar the best laid plans.

First, we must recognize local conditions by combining a comprehensive program with flexibility. If the locale is intensely nationalistic, it is no use stocking a bookstore heavily with a translation of a Western book, however good it may be, particularly if there are original works available written by less gifted yet still capable nationals. Or again, if the local church is reaching the working man, but failing to touch the professional man—or vice-versa—then it may be time to produce an alternative correspondence course, either raising the standard or simplifying the original course as the case may be. A sample survey sometimes helps.

Second, we must mobilize our fullest potential, particularly in the area of distribution, by holding more literature conferences and workshops for pastors and church members, demonstrating to them the value of literature and handing back to the local church in a large measure the responsibility of distribution. When this is done the effects are ascertainable within a given restricted area—highlighting the value of total church mobilization in distributing literature. This can also very readily awaken the local churches in the entire area to the necessity of growing if they are to remain healthy.

Third, we must not only look ahead in terms of the future development of the local church (which is primary) and its increasingly specialized literature needs, but we must also keep a weather eye open to political trends. We have no entirely accurate way of measuring political changes, but especially if the government is reactionary and at the same time vulnerable, and revolution is in the air, it would seem imperative to sell the mission press and cultivate the use of the local printers even if they are somewhat inefficient. As a general policy it is better to have the goodwill of the people and sacrifice some efficiency, than to alienate the business section of the community—not to mention the very real possibility of nationalization of all foreign assets when the new dictator puts through his "reforms."

It cannot be overemphasized that the earlier the national is incorporated into the literature program the better it is for both the ministry of literature and for the national church. An ideal evangelistic tool in the work of personal evangelism, quality literature is essential to the building up of healthy converts within the framework of a sound church structure. However, it has been noted that a national church frequently reflects the weaknesses of the older established Western church; and, by virtue of its exposure to more violent exterior forces, the national church delineates more sharply the nature of these weaknesses.

Literature at home

We need to ask ourselves two basic questions—and to answer them as honestly as we can. First, are we here

228

at home reaching into the lives and homes of those outside the traditionally conservative lower-middle class section of society? Second, are we producing sufficient quantity of Christian literature at home which by its quality is able to compete with its secular counterpart?

In their anxiety to "get the gospel out," is it possible that writers, publishers, and the general Christian public alike have not maintained the best possible standards? Much of our literature at home is of an inferior content and standard. Do we then deserve the attention we demand and even crave for the sake of proclaiming the good news?

A. W. Tozer in an outspoken editorial in *The Alliance Witness* for April 22, 1959, states bluntly, "Indeed it is hardly too much to say that illiterate religious literature has now become the earmark of evangelicalism." He goes on in a later paragraph to assert:

> The major cause of the decline in the quality of current Christian literature is not intellectual; it is spiritual. To enjoy a great religious work requires a degree of consecration to God and detachment from the world that few modern Christians have experienced. The early Christian Fathers, the mystics, the Puritans, are not hard to understand, but they inhabit the highlands where the air is crisp and rarefied and none but the God-enamored can come.

The fields of history, politics, science, the novel, and the humanities where the non-Christian and materialistic viewpoint hold almost unchallenged sway need to be breached by Christian writers. If we believe that Christ is relevant to every segment of society, every area of human life, then we must document and expound this relevance in a manner which commands a hearing. Only when the evidence is convincingly presented, using meaningful concepts, will the wisdom of God and the inadequacy of man become apparent. There is no substitute for excellence, and the truth poorly presented will seldom overcome error skillfully contrived. Sincerity is not enough. Truth has its own integrity to maintain, and God cannot concede or dilute absolute truth any more than His holy nature can tolerate sin. As God's standard of righteousness is perfection, so God's standard in art and literature is perfection, even though it may never be attained. If man had never striven for perfection, there would have been no Michelangelo, no Milton, no Bach. God is looking and calling for, not only Michelangelos, Miltons, and Bachs, but dedicated men and women who are willing to offer their "utmost for His highest."

All things to all men

God demands "our utmost" whether he calls His servants to minister to some primitive tribe or to the most intellectually sophisticated university student in the world. Though many primitive tribes remain to be reached, God has enabled dedicated men to translate the Scriptures into the vernacular for 90 per cent of the world's population. Another 5 per cent have at least part of the Word in their own tongue. We must accelerate our efforts and complete this essential task. The Wycliffe Bible Translators and numerous other missions have not only provided many tribes with the Word of God, the only authoritative instrument by which a church can be established, but in doing so they have also provided the indispensable basis of every literature program—the Bible in the vernacular. But what of our approach to the student and professional classes, the so-called "intellectuals"?

That "not many wise men after the flesh, not many mighty, not many noble, are called" (I Corinthians 1:26) is manifestly evident throughout history. And yet this statement must be taken at its face value. It says, "not *many*." And it must also be considered together with the scripture which says that "many are called but few are chosen" (Matthew 22:14). Then the fact that "not many wise . . . mighty . . . noble are called" is not surprising. But somehow we have interpreted the statement to mean that since not many are going to be saved from among the ranks of "the wise," we can leave them alone, together with the mighty and the noble, and concentrate on the "average" individual. It might be embarrassing if we discovered just how large a percentage of "the wise" are hungry, searching souls. At best it seems an arbitrary decision to relegate to a position of neglect those whom we cannot fully comprehend. One cannot help suspecting that the real reason for our inability to produce more than a trickle of quality literature is that we have been unwilling to adapt ourselves to people whom we do not understand —whom, in fact, we distrust. We have been unwilling to exercise our minds in order to gain understanding. We have frequently distrusted not merely "the wise" themselves, but the whole realm of the human mind.

While conceding that the mind unenlightened by the Spirit will never find God, yet we are bound to believe that the mind is a gift of God. We saw in an earlier chapter one of the most painful lessons which emerged from the success of the Communists in China—their profound respect for the human mind. Even the simplest and the youngest are given systematic indoctrination courses which have been highly successful—even among U.S. prisoners of war. The moral seems to be that we have underestimated the capacity of even the average human mind to understand and absorb complex data. Many missionaries working among illiterates have been confronted with the abilities of the uneducated mind, and are acutely aware that many a poverty-stricken Oriental is a profound mystic, possessing a philosophical frame of mind which would baffle most educated Westerners.

In summary we can say that the scope for literature is unlimited; its priority is essential. We must support and strengthen such valuable inter-mission literature agencies as Evangelical Literature Overseas, Moody Literature Mission, etc. On the local level we must promote co-operation and the pooling of resources for a general advance. We must be careful not to generalize on the universal efficacy of any one method. Individually we should discover whether God has given us any latent writing talent, and if He has, we should develop it. We must produce many more capable writers and journalists, as well as qualified persons for all the many literature posts which call for special gifts. There is a definite obligation for all missionary writers and literature personnel to train at least one national to take over his job after him. Such training should be tackled earnestly and systematically.

Finally, there is a personal obligation on the part of every Christian, whether he lives in Tallahassee or Timbuctoo, to distribute literature. This may mean giving (or if you are a student, recommending) books to your friends; it sometimes means handing out tracts in the market place; it could involve setting up a book counter at some Christian—or even non-Christian—conference; or it may even mean subscribing to a magazine for somebody you feel would benefit. Then, too, we must remember, that "Mr. Page" needs support just like any other missionary, and the more we give, the more his ministry multiplies. There is simply no limit to either his endurance or his fruitfulness. But we must pray continually if that fruit is to abide. Because there is often nobody to follow up each individual piece of literature bought or received, we must pray all the more that God the Holy Spirit will water the seed sown—that He will convict of sin, righteousness and judgment.

Radio

Overlooking the city and harbor of Roman Catholic Monte Carlo on the south coast of France is a radio transmitting station. Built by Adolf Hitler to broadcast the gospel of nazism around the world, the building currently houses the giant transmitters of Trans World Radio, a Christian radio station broadcasting the Christian message in twenty-eight languages around the globe. In 1956 a now famous revolt took place in Budapest. Among those who fled the Red tyrants was a brilliant Hungarian linguist. Today Trans World Radio is using his talents; the gospel is being beamed into almost every one of the Iron Curtain countries including Hungary—and even deep into Siberia. Neither a Hitler nor a Stalin nor a Khrushchev can thwart the sovereign purposes of God. For He makes even the wrath of man to praise Him (Psalm 76:10).

Radio is one of the most striking means God is using today to spread His gospel throughout the world. The history of missionary radio is a dramatic story which began little more than thirty years ago. Apart from a small station in Holland, international religious broadcasting began in 1931 with station HCJB in Quito, Ecuador. At the close of World War II, there were still only two missionary radio stations. Today, following a period of phenomenal expansion, there are more

234

than a score. Like literature, radio is a complex undertaking which requires trained technicians, researchers, engineers, producers, etc., as well as broadcasters to blanket the air-waves of the world with the gospel. The effort expended has been amply vindicated.

On any one day, more people hear the gospel today by radio than heard it during the first three centuries of the Christian era. Although some programs are substandard in quality and effectiveness in achieving a clear communication of the full message of the grace of God, the results derived from this worldwide torrent of words pouring from hundreds of transmitters are enormous. And not only is radio an evangelistic medium. Many a program is designed to teach the Scriptures, nurture isolated Christians, challenge the careless, and bring the Christian message of hope and strength to the burdened.

Observations on the effectiveness and usefulness of radio are many:

1. People today are curious about the gospel, but reluctant or unable to attend churches and admit their curiosity. Social, religious, and family pressures hold many back. Yet, in the privacy of their homes or automobiles, they not only can but do listen to Christian radio programs. In Latin America the educated, nominal Roman Catholic and in America the hungry-hearted Jew represent two sizeable classes of people who are increasingly being reached through radio programs. Iron and bamboo curtain countries

235

contain many people who secretly listen to short wave programs beamed from places as remote as Ecuador and Manila, Korea and Ceylon. People in remote Arctic regions, on isolated islands in the sea, in innumerable out of the way places, and shut-ins everywhere are hearing of the nearness and dearness of God's grace in Christ. It can be affirmed without fear of contradiction that through radio literally millions have heard the gospel for the first time. It is not without reason that Satan has tried in every conceivable way to hinder this type of outreach.

2. Radio programs can be repeated and rebroadcast at times when no other means of communication could work as effectively. Although initial costs are high, in a number of countries it is possible to erect "Christian" stations which prepare high-level programs of a balanced nature including a variety of musical forms, educational services, news and weather reports, and community promotion, interspersed with a good percentage of strictly Christian programs. In many foreign countries these Christian-operated stations are quite popular, and afford local citizens relief from the steady barrage of jazz-plus-commercials-plus-politics that is the monotonous output of the average local shoe-string-managed station.

3. Radio can readily develop a regular constituency by means of "portable pastors." These are pre-tuned receiving sets, generally battery operated, which are distributed to village churches or installed in central

buildings where no churches have as yet been established. This method has had notable success in the Philippines and in Korea, not only in evangelistic outreach, but also in conserving the results of evangelism through radio schools of the Bible, and Bible correspondence courses tied in to Bible study programs, etc.

4. Radio is essentially an inexpensive operation in terms of the number of people it reaches for Christ. On a per capita basis the cost is infinitesimal. It compares extremely favorably with the cost of maintaining an individual missionary overseas and reaches far more people and more frequently, day in and day out, than he could ever hope to reach by direct contact. And yet, it has been demonstrated that in certain countries where radio coverage has been good but missionary coverage poor, no strong local churches have resulted. This points up radio's great weakness: it divorces the voice from the personal presence. It cannot engage in dialogue and interaction between witness and recipient. For this reason radio is not to be regarded as a substitute for the direct evangelistic approach made by individuals, either in personal witness or in the evangelistic meeting. But radio is a highly effective prejudice-removing, interest-creating aid to evangelism.

5. Radio is the stepping stone to television. In such countries as Japan where every major city has at least one TV station and Tokyo at least six, and where radio programs are currently bringing at least one hundred

people monthly into contact with local churches for the first time, Christian leaders are beginning to feel that they must increasingly invade the TV field. As the appetite of a people develops for this sophisticated medium of communication, Christians who have already mastered the use of radio are the ones most likely to move in to this new field.

The Christian who considers this type of service needs special training in the field of religious journalism, since most radio programs are carefully prepared beforehand, then read or memorized. He should be a student of the human heart, since a message with warmth and human appeal is especially needed to overcome the depersonalization of the voice so inherent in all radio outreach.

Conclusion

"For every four persons on earth in 1950, there are today five. For every five today, in forty years there will probably be ten. In the past half minute alone, about 90 babies will have been born into the world; only 60 persons will have died, leaving a net increase of 30, or 1 every second." [5] These are the authoritative facts as given by Eugene Black, President of the World Bank. Place such statistics alongside the fact that before the end of the year, world population will have exceeded 3 billion, and then compare these figures with

---

5. *U.S. News & World Report*, L (May 8, 1961), 82.

the fact that there are approximately 42,000 active professional missionaries in the world today. Without suggesting that the task of world evangelism rests with these 42,000, it is nevertheless obvious that we must employ every means available. Without literature and radio, the task would be humanly impossible. But by the grace of God we have been given the means to meet this colossal challenge.

"Give me twenty-six lead soldiers," Benjamin Franklin once said, "and I will conquer the world." Never has this claim been so close to the truth. And yet God's method is still men. Whenever and wherever radio and literature become ends in themselves rather than means—God's blessing is withheld. Backed by the believing prayers of God's people, radio and literature are powerful instruments for proclaiming the full counsel of God. It is, however, an almighty God himself who has promised that "my word . . . that goes forth from my mouth . . . shall not return to me empty,"

> but it shall accomplish that which I purpose,
> and prosper in the thing for which I sent it.
>   (Isaiah 55:11)

239

Chapter 12: **Looking Forward**

FIELD MARSHAL MONTGOMERY WRITES, "The British army entered the Second World War in 1939 admirably organized and equipped to fight the 1914 war and with the wrong officers at the top." He adds, "It was totally unfit to fight a first-class war on the continent of Europe."[1] Field Marshal Montgomery's point is quite simply that, although the men who comprised the army were first-class material, the leadership of the army, its weapons, and its strategy were hopelessly obsolete and inadequate.

This was true not only of the British army, but equally of the French army. The image of the trench warfare of the First World War, with its limited military objectives and slow advances, led to the construction of the Maginot line and a view of warfare that was entirely defensive rather than offensive. No one who

---

1. *The Memoirs of Field Marshal Montgomery* (Cleveland: World Publishing Company, 1958), pp. 37, 46.

lived through the dark days of 1940 in western Europe and Great Britain will soon forget what a heavy price was paid in human lives and suffering for these very mistakes. The Anglo-French armies were totally unprepared for the fluid and fast-moving tactics of the German panzers.

Since 1945 sweeping changes have taken place which have vitally affected the outlook and living conditions of the majority of countries throughout the world. In the relatively short span of sixteen years, changes of colossal magnitude have transformed the very nature of the world in which we live in undreamed of ways. Today there is a very real possibility that our missionary leadership may find itself at the head of a missionary arm that is "admirably organized and equipped" to evangelize the world as it was prior to 1939, or at best 1945, but totally out of touch and unprepared to minister realistically and effectively in the world as we find it today.

The Supreme Strategist

More and more leaders of various missions are recognizing that it is not enough to have large numbers of sincere and dedicated Christians working throughout the world for the cause of Jesus Christ. There is real need for imaginative planning based upon penetrating insights, that the Church may make its impact upon this generation. We can be thankful that God in His wisdom has given to His Church men with sensitivity to

241

the world situation. The sanctified imagination so needful to the missionary enterprise of the Church of Christ, the ability to demonstrate and transmit the crusading spirit on the offensive, the capacity to pioneer fresh advances and reject outmoded methods—all these must be cultivated by the twentieth-century missionary leader.

In such a context there is one pre-eminent fact to be kept in mind. There is only one strategist in the Church of Jesus Christ, and He is the Holy Spirit of God. It is imperative that we use every scrap of information we are able to obtain, and that we mobilize our finest resources in the cause of world evangelization. But when we have done this we need to recognize that there is only One who "searches everything, even the depths of God. For what person knows a man's thoughts except the spirit of the man which is in him? So also no one comprehends the thoughts of God except the Spirit of God" (I Corinthians 2:10b, 11). It behooves us to cultivate deep humility of mind and action as we consider the work of the Lord throughout the world and Christ's purpose for His Church. By human standards it may be relatively simple for us to determine what are the "important" and the "unimportant" types of missionary work, but our ways are not His ways and His evaluation may be the opposite of ours. In the final analysis a man or woman goes to a particular mission field, not because he likes that particular type of work, nor because he fits in with an imaginative man-made

242

strategy, but because he receives his marching orders from the Commander-in-Chief of the Army. A missionary working faithfully for thirty years in some Muslim country and seeing virtually nothing in terms of results may be a failure so far as the strategy of man is concerned, but a brilliant success in the eyes of God, and His is the evaluation that counts. This does not relieve us, however, of the responsibility of seeking to discern the signs of our times. We must employ our God-given intelligence in assessing the needs of our day and fully exploit the means that God has placed at our disposal.

Today's Trends and the Church's Ministry

In the preceding pages we have attempted to focus attention upon some of the far-reaching developments of the past decade or so, the outstanding characteristics of the world today, and their impact upon world evangelization. It is highly possible for any one of us to devote too much attention to a particular detail of God's work or of God's doctrine. Most of us know that a caricature is produced by taking one detail and enlarging it out of all proportion to the rest of the picture and thus making it grotesque. It is important for us to endeavor to see the whole picture and not just one small part of it.

What are some of the trends and characteristics of our day that are bound to affect profoundly the whole course of the ministry of the Church in the next few years? We shall recapitulate these trends and summarize some of the steps the Church must take if we are going to serve our generation successfully in the will of God.

Hostility

For several centuries the Church has lived in a relatively peaceful and privileged environment in which she has often been welcomed, respected, or at the worst merely tolerated. Living in the comparative tranquility of the West, it is difficult for us to understand that the era of privilege has definitely passed. It is probable that more Christians have been killed for their love for Jesus Christ in the last twenty-five years than in the rest of the history of the Church combined. We are living in a day when the Church has to earn the right to speak and when she must bear in mind that her members must be prepared to suffer for the cause of Jesus Christ.

The role of North America

Two-thirds of all Protestant missionaries in the world come from North America, and an even larger proportion of the financial contribution to Protestant missions comes from this continent. In terms of resources, the North American has a vital and exceedingly difficult role to play. There has probably never been a period in the history of the Church when leadership needed to be exercised with such humility and tact. Instead of ex-

244

pressing regret at our loss of status, we can thank God that the political situation in the world demands a compliance with the spirit of the New Testament. Our leadership must fit the pattern of the Apostle Paul who was prepared to be a servant and a slave of all that he might please Jesus Christ and be a blessing to others.

Population explosion

Enough has been written on this for us to do no more than mention it. Yet it is at once the greatest problem and challenge of our day and one that has far-reaching and immediate implications for the Church. Our present population to be reached with the gospel is at least nine times the number of people who lived at the time of Jesus Christ. By 2,000 A.D. this number will have doubled. Whereas we have nine people to reach for every one in Paul's day, in less than forty years we shall have eighteen to reach. Statistics are certainly not an overriding factor in the counsels of God and of His Church, but we dare not ignore the fact that we have mushrooming responsibilities, while at the present rate of expansion the Church is not even succeeding in holding her own.

The growth of the cities

The significant and increasing trend of previously rural communities to move into the cities is a factor that we must face. Presenting us at once with unparalleled opportunities but also with immense difficulties, this may be one of the acid tests of the true spiritual effectiveness of the Church of Jesus Christ. If we are not able to make the gospel relevant to the sprawling urban masses, then we shall be undermining the whole effort of contemporary world evangelism.

The student classes

The phenomenal increase in education and the emergence of a huge student class should serve to stimulate the Church into a re-examination of her own spiritual resources and her frequent tendency to withdraw from the intellectual battlefield. We cannot willfully leave millions of students, many of them groping and searching, without a clear-cut message at this crucial moment in history.

The fact of revolution

Perhaps no other single fact has so influenced the presentation of the gospel in our generation than the revolutionary ferment that is so characteristic of our world today. Clearly there is no simple answer to the problem. Equally apparent to many is the fact that Christians throughout the world need to become far more aware and sensitive to the tensions within society. It must be conceded that there are very few issues on which the corporate Church is justified in formulating views and expressing resolutions, for it is precisely this tendency that has often led the Church to become an

246

organizational and temporal entity rather than a spiritual power. But the individual Christian should be sensitive and articulate in the realm of social problems, although he must subordinate his activity and concern to the priority of spiritual principles.

The growth of literacy

Throughout the world the Church has initiated great literacy programs and has placed in the hands of millions the ability to read and understand the written word. This of itself is obviously good. But tragically, as the Communists themselves have said, "The Church has taught the people to read, but it is we who have provided them with the reading materials."

It is only relatively recently that the Church has begun to rise to the challenge of providing for new literates the literature that can satisfy their spiritual and intellectual appetites. The power of the printed page is incalculable, and he who reaches the minds of the masses through this medium in the coming years will have won, to a large extent, their hearts also.

The resurgence of sophisticated religions

While a great deal of attention is usually focused upon the animistic and primitive tribes, in the area of religion a far more extensive challenge is to be found in the more sophisticated religions of the East such as Hinduism and Buddhism and Islam.

247

Our day is seeing a resurgence of energy on the part of almost every major religion; a resurgence that seemed utterly improbable ten or even fifteen years ago. On the part of all these religions, there is renewed and feverish activity to strengthen and confirm the faithful as well as to embrace fresh converts and extend their influence. This resurgence of energy may be traced to a number of diverse factors. At least partly, it may be attributed to the very success of the Christian mission in various countries; it may also be traced to a sensing that the impact of the West has weakened the inherited faith of many, leading them to a fresh evaluation and concerted effort to make their faith relevant for the twentieth century.

For instance, sweeping social reforms impinging on traditional Islamic practice have been carried out in some Muslim communities, of which Tunisia is a good example. Throughout Latin America the Roman Catholic Church, aware of the tremendous losses it has sustained among its followers and particularly among the professional classes, is making vast new attempts to change its centuries-old methods of working and to mobilize all available resources in an attempt to recapture Latin America for the Roman church. The fact that in many cases these religions have borrowed and adapted from methods used by the Christian church is often an indication of how successful the Christian mission has been in those countries long regarded as the sole preserve of another religion.

The decline of the white man

That the white man still has a great contribution to make to the spread of the gospel throughout the world is questioned by very few church leaders, even in the young, non-white churches. Nevertheless the political and social emancipation of the non-white races places the ministry of the white man in a completely new perspective.

At least one mission has compiled a list of missionaries who are unable or unwilling to adapt themselves to this changed situation and to serve with meekness and humility under the leadership of non-whites. Thus their service with the mission must be terminated. It is to be wished that many more missions were as determined to eradicate those individuals who cling to color barriers. Sadly, even while believing that a man's heart is the important thing in God's sight, many of us remain strangely preoccupied with the pigment of his skin.

The Church's weapons

Not since the days when the Caliph's armies subjugated nation after nation, expanding the Muslim Empire's boundaries not only clear across Africa and the Middle East, but also deep into Europe to occupy the whole of Spain and extend into France, has the Church faced such a dire threat to her existence as she faces today in conflict with atheistic Marxism.

249

That this is a battle to death, few will deny. But concerning the weapons to be used in that battle, there is a wide disagreement. Unfortunately a large segment of the Church has been utterly unable to learn from the Muslim conquests of centuries ago. The Muslims extended their kingdom by the sword, and a Church strong in political influence but weak in spiritual power thought that the answer was to attack Islam with her own weapons. Thus were mounted a succession of crusades whose soldiers wore a cross upon their armor, but whose mission was a carnal and futile one. Today there are those in the Church who feel that the weapons of the Church are the American marine and the American dollar. However legitimate these may be in the service of a nation, they have no place in the armory of the Church.

To attack Satan with material and physical weapons alone is like attacking a modern tank with a can opener.

> For though we live in the world we are not carrying on
> a worldly war, for the weapons of our warfare are not
> worldly but have divine power to destroy strongholds
> (II Corinthians 10:3, 4).

This solemn fact should lead us to a new sense of urgency in the fulfilling of the commission of Jesus Christ. In viewing the accelerating tensions of the whole world and the possibility of global warfare breaking out, every serious-minded child of God must wonder how much time remains to accomplish the work at hand.

In such troubled and uncertain days, what an indescribable comfort it is to the Christian to know that his hope is not centered in any man or council of men but in the Lord of Glory himself. The whole of history is moving toward its consummation in Jesus Christ. The fact that our Lord is going to return, and that the end is going to come, affords us great comfort—but no escape from responsibility for the enormous task that lies at hand. We are commanded to make the most of the time—a command which accentuates the sense of urgency arising from a study of world events. The task is overwhelming and the time is short. We have been entrusted with a privilege which no other generation since the Apostles has been given. We dare not be fearful, neither must we slacken in zeal in prosecuting the supreme mission of the Church to our generation.

Today and Tomorrow

One conclusion is inescapable. The lateness of the hour reinforces the commission of our Lord and should lead us to an all-out attempt to reach the world for Christ. This is not the hobby of a few enthusiasts, nor yet an optional extra; this is *the* mission of the Church of Jesus Christ. We do not want nor do we need to be missionary fanatics, but neither do we wish to be like those who in the days of Noah "were eating and drinking, marrying and giving in marriage, until the day

251

when Noah entered the ark, and they did not know
until the flood came and swept them all away. . . ."
For, "so will be the coming of the Son of man" (Matthew 24:38–39).

He is waiting with long patience
　　For His crowning day,
For that kingdom which shall never
　　Pass away.

And till every tribe and nation
　　Bow before His throne,
He expecteth loyal service
　　From His own.

He expecteth; but He heareth
　　Still the bitter cry
From earth's millions, "Come and help us,
　　For we die."

He expecteth; doth He see us
　　Busy here and there,
Heedless of those pleading accents
　　Of despair?

Shall we, dare we, disappoint Him?
　　Brethren, let us rise!
He who died for us is watching
　　From the skies;

Watching till His royal banner
　　Floateth far and wide,

252

Till he seeth of His travail—
Satisfied!

—*Alice J. Janvrin*

One of the first principles in modern warfare is that there must be an attempt to mobilize the resources of the whole nation. Total war demands total commitment. This is as true for the Church as it is for a nation. Inevitably it demands sacrifice, not merely from those who become part of the fighting services, but from all who are called to support the effort by living and working in the homeland. Christians have yet to apply this principle in the spiritual warfare in which we are engaged.

Such warfare demands that we define objectives and allocate adequate resources to obtain them. This involves the determination of priorities, for there will never be enough time and resources to accomplish everything, and certain less essential things must be surrendered to obtain the all-important things.

In endeavoring to establish priorities in our missionary enterprise for tomorrow, we must consider not merely what seems to be the most productive in terms of future results and the strategic interest of the Church, but also those areas we have previously neglected. No list of priorities will command universal agreement, but certain emphases must characterize our missionary effort of the next decade, if we have a decade left in which to work.

253

Total mobilization

As we have previously pointed out, this task demands the mobilizing, not merely of the resources of the Church in the Western world, but also the resources of the churches in other countries. This is essential if we are to meet the challenge of the population explosion, or in the event that anti-Western hostility causes a drastic cut-back in the missionary activity of the Western nations.

Such a mobilization of resources would have an important effect on the churches involved, as well as on the areas to be evangelized. Among Brazil's 70 million there are two million registered Protestants. It would seem that enough of these should be mature, educated, and devoted Christians to be able to accept the major responsibility for the evangelization of the 50 to 75,000 (according to Dr. Eugene Nida) aboriginal people of the Amazon River Basin. It is not merely the tribes that need this ministry; the Church in Brazil needs it. A church that does not have a missionary vision for the people of its own community, and whose vision does not reach out to embrace those beyond its own geographic boundaries, is a stagnant church—one likely to have its witness terminated by its own Lord. That such a fate is not impossible is clear from the remarks of our Lord addressed to the church at Ephesus:

254

Remember then from what you have fallen, repent and
do the works you did at first. If not, I will come to you
and remove your lampstand from its place, unless you
repent (Revelation 2:5).

The history of the early church in North Africa, which,
though it produced giants such as Augustine, lacked
missionary vision and thus vanished in the path of the
Muslim invaders, is a grim warning to all self-centered
churches.

Such a missionary vision is only imparted by sound
teaching, backed by prayer. Our aim must be to present
to every Christian in the world today a twofold vision.
First of all, there is the vision of our Lord himself in
His authority and in His glory commissioning every
single one of His children to be a witness to himself and
His resurrection. The second aspect of the vision that
we should seek to impart will be that of a world that
Christ loved and for whom He gave himself as a ransom.

The role of the layman

Implicit in the first priority is the mobilization of the
almost limitless energies and skills of laymen throughout the world. There has been far too great a tendency to rely on the efforts of "professionals" in the
ministry of the Church. Believing as we do in the
priesthood of all believers, and the fact that every one
who names Jesus Christ as Lord and Savior is indwelt

255

by the Spirit of God, there is obviously no limit to what may be accomplished by men and women with a boundless faith in Jesus Christ. As has been pointed out elsewhere, this lesson has been clearly demonstrated by the work of many Pentecostal groups. Perhaps one of the most striking illustrations of this is the work going on in many parts of inland Colombia today. One man alone, barely literate, formally uneducated, and because of marital tangles developed before becoming a Christian, not even a church member, in a period of three or four years has directly and indirectly been responsible for the conversion of between 1,000 and 1,500 of his fellow-Colombians.

It will not be God's will to use everybody in this exceedingly dramatic way. But we dare not limit the Lord by our lack of faith. It is to be trusted that the very pressures of the day in which we live may drive us back to embrace principles clearly taught in the New Testament. This will involve much work in selection, training, and above all the will power, humility, and faith to practice the art of delegation.

Literature

Perhaps the most heartening development in the evangelical church in the last decade has been the vigor that has characterized missionary literature. After many, many years of uncoordinated and occasionally competitive literature efforts by individual mission boards and groups, there has been an increased trend toward greater coordination, and the achievements have indeed been remarkable. When one considers that the Evangelical Literature Fellowship of India, in a period of seven years, produced nine hundred different titles of literature in fifteen languages, one can only be thrilled and grateful for such an accomplishment. Nevertheless, far from encouraging us to relax our efforts, this should rather stimulate us to see what can be done in ever-increasing measure and with greater efficiency.

Many mission boards have come to the conclusion that they should aim at allocating ten per cent of their personnel and ten per cent of their budget for the cause of literature. It may not be quite so glamorous to send money to a mission board for literature as it is to send money to support a pleasing personality. But in facing the facts of twentieth-century life, we must recognize the need of expanding and improving our literature ministry. To this end we shall need a stream of well-trained, dedicated young people and the sacrificial giving of countless numbers of the Lord's children.

Developing leadership

Serious attention must obviously be given to our present methods of training Christian leaders. In modern warfare an increasingly large emphasis is being placed upon new and unorthodox forms of training. In all too

257

many recent conflicts, conventionally trained troops have been outmaneuvered and outfought by those well-versed in guerrilla tactics and other irregular forces.

The time has surely come when we must ask ourselves whether our existing methods of training leadership are producing the kind of men that we need in the total warfare of our day and generation. A soldier is not made in a classroom alone; he becomes one on the battlefield.

Perhaps the most strategic work for many of us would be to select a small group of individuals to work with in order to teach them, not only by word but also by example, the true principles of spiritual leadership in spiritual warfare. Such a ministry is far more exacting than mere classroom teaching, but it is a responsibility that we dare not shun if we are to produce the men and women who will count for God in the world today. Instruction and exhortation are not enough; we need demonstration. There is no substitute for the instructor's taking the disciple on the battlefield and teaching by example.

Reaching the students

One of our top priorities today is the reaching of the student classes of the world. Relatively large numbers of missionaries have been called by God to work among primitive tribes, and in many cases their work has represented the very best type of missionary enterprise, combining a willingness to accept physical privations, acute danger, and the most primitive standard of living, while using advanced methods of language reduction and technological skill. We must pray that others in the Church will demonstrate such qualities of imagination and daring in reaching the students of the world for Jesus Christ.

In stressing the urgency of student work, however, we are not suggesting that these two types of work are in competition with each other. In fact they are complementary. We do not need one or the other, but both. But because the student class has been largely neglected by evangelical missions, special efforts need to be made by leaders of existing missionary organizations to set aside suitable and experienced men and women for the task of reaching the students. Many missionary leaders are concerned and are taking action to meet this need. But as yet very few in the home churches have the burden for prayer that is desperately needed if this strategic theater of spiritual warfare is to be successfully invaded and conquered.

The cities for Christ

For some the challenge of working in cities may represent the acid test of obedience as well as of imagination. Many of the world's cities are ugly, sordid places, and few would choose to live and work there out of any natural desire. It has already been indicated that to attack the cities will be an expensive business in terms of finance and will involve much toil and self-

259

denial on the part of dedicated missionaries. But we dare not flinch in the face of this enormous task, for at stake are huge possibilities both for success and for failure. If we lose the cities, we lose the world.

When every resource of man's ingenuity, experience, skill, and energy has been pressed into the task of reaching the world for Christ, we must recognize with true humility that we could have the most dedicated of human beings, in vast numbers, embodying the latest resources of skill and education, and be led by the most imaginative men with the soundest possible judgment, but that all would be totally and completely useless so far as spiritual warfare is concerned simply because our warfare and our weapons are not worldly. In the final analysis it should be obvious to every Christian who is able to discern the central spiritual issues in the history of the Church, and who has an understanding of the things of the Lord, that only a sovereign intervention of God, by His Holy Spirit, in the affairs of men can possibly meet the challenge of our world. It was ever thus and will continue to be so. The true man of God is ever a realist. We must not underestimate the danger and urgency of the time in which we live. Let us confess our own weakness and lack of ability to meet the situation, and may we as members of the Church of Christ pray with heartfelt urgency that God will visit His Church in a new way in these latter days. First, let us pray for a sensitivity to sin that springs from a view of the holiness of God, and then go forth in utter and complete dependence upon Him, expecting great things from God and attempting great things for God.

We are creatures of imbalance and usually we think either in terms of the spiritual or in terms of methods and technique. We must together bend to the task every faculty that we possess and every human resource at our disposal and yet, deep down and in absolute honesty, recognize that without His touch all is vain. We need to ask, not so much that He bless our labors, as that He dominate us in our thinking and in our planning. It has been said, "Only one life, 'twill soon be past; only what's done for Christ will last." But it is more accurate to say, not merely that which is done for Jesus will last, but that which is done by Jesus.

O Breath of Life, come sweeping through us,
Revive Thy Church with life and power;
O Breath of Life, come, cleanse, renew us,
And fit Thy Church to meet this hour.

O Wind of God, come bend us, break us,
Till humbly we confess our need;
Then in Thy tenderness remake us,
Revive, restore; for this we plead.

O Breath of Love, come breathe within us,
Renewing thought and will and heart;
Come, Love of Christ, afresh to win us,
Revive Thy Church in every part.

261

Revive us, Lord! Is zeal abating
While harvest fields are vast and white?
Revive us, Lord, the world is waiting,
Equip Thy Church to spread the light.
—*Bessie Porter Head*

. . . David . . . served his own generation by the
will of God . . . .

—Acts 13:36

As life is action and passion, it is required of a man that
he should share the passion and action of his time, at
the peril of being judged not to have lived.

—Oliver Wendell Holmes, Jr.

A Brief Bibliography

The following list suggests a few of the significant contributions to the literature on various subjects considered in this book. Not all of the selected titles reflect evangelical points of view, and some are admittedly controversial. Their inclusion here is intended hopefully to stimulate thought in areas which the reader may wish to explore further.

Revolution

ADENEY, DAVID H. *The Unchanging Commission.* Chicago: Inter-Varsity Press, 1955. Chicago: Moody Press, Colportage Library.

MANIKAM, RAJAH B. (ed.). *Christianity and the Asian Revolution.* Madras and New York: Friendship Press, 1954.

MASTON, T. B. *Christianity and World Issues.* New York: The Macmillan Co., 1957.

PATON, DAVID M. *Christian Missions and the Judgment of God*. London: S.C.M. Press, Ltd., 1953.

SOPER, EDMUND DAVISON. *The Philosophy of the Christian World Mission*. Nashville: Abingdon Press, 1951.

Nationalism

HAYES, CARLTON J. H. *Nationalism: A Religion*. New York: The Macmillan Co., 1960.

KRAEMER, HENDRIK. *World Cultures and World Religions*. Philadelphia: The Westminster Press, 1960.

WARREN, MAX A. C. *Caesar the Beloved Enemy*. London: S.C.M. Press, Ltd., 1955.

Communism

BRUNNER, EMIL. *Communism, Capitalism and the Social Order*. London: Lutterworth Press, 1940.

CHAMBERS, WHITTAKER. *Witness*. New York: Random House, 1952.

DEVANANDAN, P. D., and THOMAS, M. M. *Communism and the Social Revolution in India: A Christian Interpretation*. Calcutta: Y.M.C.A. Publishing House, 1953.

HOOK, SIDNEY. *Marx and the Marxists*. New York: D. Van Nostrand Co., Inc., 1955.

HUNT, R. N. CAREW. *The Theory and Practice of Communism*. New York: The Macmillan Co., 1957.

NAFT, S. *Questions for Communists*. New York: New Leader Press, 1951.

266

Church and Communism

BENNETT, JOHN C. *Christianity and Communism Today*. New York: Association Press, 1960.

Church of Scotland: General Assembly Commission. *The Church Under Communism*. New York: Philosophical Library, 1953.

DEKOSTER, LESTER. *All Ye That Labor*. Grand Rapids: Wm. B. Eerdman's Publishing Company, 1956.

PRICE, FRANK WILSON. *Marx Meets Christ*. Philadelphia: The Westminster Press, 1957.

SHUSTER, GEORGE N. *Religion Behind the Iron Curtain*. New York: The Macmillan Co., 1954.

WEST, CHARLES C. *Outside the Camp*. New York: Doubleday & Co., Inc., 1959.

Ecumenical Movement

BAVINCK, J. H. *The Impact of Christianity on the Non-Christian World*. Grand Rapids: Wm. B. Eerdman's Publishing Co., 1948.

HOGG, WILLIAM RICHEY. *Ecumenical Foundations*. New York: Harper & Brothers, 1952.

KRAEMER, HENDRIK. *The Christian Message in a Non-Christian World*. New York: Harper & Brothers, 1938.

Cities

Latin America Mission. *Evangelism in Depth*. Chicago: Moody Press, 1961.

Students

ADENEY, DAVID H. *Christian Students in a Communist Society.* Chicago: Inter-Varsity Press, 1951.

HUMMEL, CHARLES E. *Campus Christian Witness.* Chicago: Inter-Varsity Press, 1958.

POLLOCK, J. C. *A Cambridge Movement.* London: John Murray, 1953.

WALSH, CHAD. *Campus Gods on Trial.* Revised edition. New York: The Macmillan Co., 1962.

Literature and Radio

CHIRGWIN, A. M. *The Bible in World Evangelism.* New York: Friendship Press, 1954.

DIFFENDORFER, RALPH E. *Christian Literature in the Mission World.* New York: International Missionary Council, 1946.

GILLES, JOHN. *A Primer for Christian Broadcasters.* Chicago: Moody Press, 1955.

JONES, CLARENCE W. *Radio, the New Missionary.* Chicago: Moody Press, 1946.

LAUBACH, FRANK C. and ROBERT S. *Toward World Literacy.* Syracuse: Syracuse University Press, 1960.

NIDA, EUGENE A. *God's Word in Man's Language.* New York: Harper & Brothers, 1952.

URE, RUTH. *The Highway of Print.* New York: Friendship Press, 1946.

268

WARREN, RUTH URE. *Literacy*. London: Edinburgh House Press, 1956.

Strategy

DAVIS, J. MERLE. *New Buildings on Old Foundations*. London and New York: International Missionary Council, 1947.

FELTON, RALPH A. *Hope Rises from the Land*. New York: Friendship Press, 1955. (Agricultural missions)

HEILBRONER, ROBERT L. *The Future as History*. New York: Harper & Brothers, 1959.

History's Lessons for Tomorrow's Mission. Miscellaneous Essays. Geneva: World's Student Christian Federation, 1960.

McGAVRAN, DONALD. *How Churches Grow*. London: World Dominion Press, 1959. New York: Friendship Press.